THE APERITIF COMPANION

A Connoisseur's Guide to the World of Aperitifs

THE
APERITIF
COMPANION

A Connoisseur's Guide to the World of Aperitifs

ANDREW JONES

KNICKERBOCKER

Published by Knickerbocker Press
276 Fifth Avenue
New York, New York 10001

This edition produced for sales in the U.S.A.,
its territories and dependencies only.

A QUINTET BOOK

ISBN 1-57715-028-7

This book was designed and produced by
Quintet Publishing Limited
6 Blundell Street
London N7 9BH

Creative Director: Richard Dewing
Art Director: Silke Braun
Designer: Ian Hunt
Project Editor: Julie Carbonara
Editors: Julie Carbonara, Jane Hurd-Cosgrave
Photographer: Adrian Swift

Typeset in Great Britain by
Central Southern Typesetters, Eastbourne
Manufactured in Singapore by United Graphic Pte Ltd
Printed in Singapore by Star Standard Industries Pte Ltd

CONTENTS

AUTHOR'S ACKNOWLEDGEMENTS

The writing of this book would not have been possible without widespread support from the international aperitif producers. They have been constructive in their suggestions and responsive to questions and requests. There are no organisations that concentrate solely on the promotion of aperitifs, and so this cooperation has been of paramount importance.

Most thanks should be reserved for my wife, Branwen, who has co-ordinated the content, corrected my wayward grammar and made many positive suggestions. Additionally, I would like to extend my gratitude to my editor, Julie Carbonara, for her tireless efforts which have covered everything from chasing queries and samples across numerous countries to the scrupulous work of the final edit.

PART ONE

THE STORY OF APERITIFS

INTRODUCTION

WHAT IS AN APERITIF?

An aperitif is a drink usually taken before a meal to stimulate the appetite. The English-language word "aperitif" has its origins in the French *apéritif* and the Italian *aperitivo*.

Nowadays, with the prospering of international trade, a wide range of drinks – from champagne to Southern Comfort – are enjoyed as aperitifs, with many a glass of Chardonnay fulfilling the same role. Although the categories or styles of drinks included in *The Aperitif Companion* might provoke some argument, in general, only those that have been traditionally considered aperitifs have been chosen. Some consumers may claim that certain entries are actually "digestifs" (after-dinner drinks), but this is by no means consistent. For example, in some regions of Italy, the bitters Cynar is drunk as an aperitif (before the meal), while in much of Germany, consumers will swear to its digestive benefits after a meal.

Confronted with the vast array of aperitifs available, attempting to classify them could prove a complicated and hazardous task. However, they can be divided broadly into two main categories: wine- and spirit-based aperitifs.

WINE-BASED APERITIFS

Wine-based aperitifs were originally developed in southern Europe, where many local wines were of poor quality. This was resolved by adding brandy, herbs, and spices to provide fortification and enhance flavor. As this practice developed, other styles of aperitifs emerged, including fortified, natural wines with no added herbs or spices. Among these are the muscats of southern France, sherry from Spain, Madeira and port from Portugal, and Commandaria from Cyprus. Montilla from Spain is an interesting exception, as it is similar in character to some sherries, but is one of the few unfortified, wine-based aperitifs. Vermouth, which is flavored with secret recipes of herbs and spices, (including *vermud* or wormwood extract, from which its name derives) was one of the most important wine-based, fortified aperitifs to develop, with successful brands like Cinzano and Martini in Italy and Noilly Prat in France. Aromatized wines, such as Dubonnet, are similar; these were originally based on quinine, as opposed to wormwood. They also are wine-based, fortified with spirits, and flavored with herbs and spices.

Although the exact, secret recipes of all the famous brands are surrounded by considerable security, known ingredients include melissa and thyme (for added aroma); cumin and nutmeg (to provide seasoning); cilantro (coriander), angelica, cardamom, cloves, mace, and myrrh.

Some of the herbs and spices used to flavor
wine-based aperitifs

SPIRIT-BASED APERITIFS

Spirit-based aperitifs have developed into two main styles, bitters and pastis, each of which have very different backgrounds. Bitters originated in the Netherlands, as the Dutch had access to many exotic herbs and spices through their colonies, and could therefore produce spirits inexpensively. The term "bitters" is self-explanatory, as these spirit-based aperitifs are often flavored with predominantly bitter-tasting herbs and spices, and are usually consumed with mixers. Campari is the most popular bitters, with the artichoke-flavored Cynar also boasting a large following. Bitters are said to be especially good for settling the stomach immediately prior to or just after food.

The roots of the yellow gentian give Suze its distinctive flavor

Pastis originated from two sources, the ancient Greek world and the Moorish-occupied southern Europe – long before the creation of spirits – and in both instances, they were simply aniseed-based drinks diluted with water. Pastis covers a wide range of aniseed drinks, from ouzo in Greece and Cyprus to the classic French Pernod. Ricard, while appearing to belong to the same category, is licorice-based, and a relatively modern version of a traditional drink from Marseilles. However, all pastis, whatever their denomination, become opaque and milky when water is added.

Another small group of spirit-based aperitifs is the gentian-flavored drinks, of which Suze is the most popular brand. The root of the yellow gentian plant (*Gentiana lutea*) is used in an infusion, which is then blended with purified, neutral alcohol. Its naturally bitter taste is balanced by adding herbs and spices.

OTHER TYPES OF APERITIF

There are further kinds of aperitifs that do not fit comfortably into any category. These include Pineau des Charentes, from the Cognac region of France, made by adding young cognac to pure-grape juice before it ferments; Ratafia, similar in style to Pineau, which is still found in the Champagne and Burgundy regions, but is increasingly rare; Guignolet, a cherry-based aperitif from Western France; and Advocaat, from the Netherlands, which is made from brandy and egg yolks.

Such divisions can neither be totally consistent nor straightforward, and although *The Aperitif Companion* does not attempt any kind of official classification, the purpose of the categories is to give a basic guide to readers. However, even the most experienced experts admit that such divisions can be rather arbitrary at the best of times.

Ingredients as diverse as black currants, cherries, eggs, and grapes go into the making of different types of aperitifs

BASIC PRODUCTION METHODS

Both wine-based aperitifs and spirit-based bitters have the same general production methods. The first step is to select and weigh the herbs and spices, some of which will be macerated (soaked) in neutral alcohol, and others steeped in water (infused). The macerations are then left to soak, sometimes for several weeks, while the infusion is brewed within a day or two, somewhat like tea. Later, the resulting liquids are drawn off, and are then blended with either the base wine or base spirit before other ingredients, such as neutral alcohol, purified water, and a sugar solution are added.

The way it is: giant containers for the maceration of herbs

Pastis production involves a maceration of aniseed, herbs, and spices (such as cilantro, nutmeg, and licorice) in neutral alcohol for around three weeks. If it follows the Marseilles tradition, licorice plays a more prominent role. The concentrate is then blended with further alcohol, raw-sugar cane, and water.

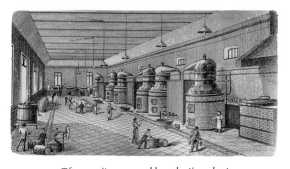

The way it was: an old production plant

THE HISTORY AND EVOLUTION OF APERITIFS

Who drank the first aperitif, and when? Was it in Jerusalem, in Biblical days, when a band of charitable women were known to have given wine, flavored with various herbs, as a medicine to the sick and dying? Although its use may not qualify as an aperitif, the basic drink is very similar to vermouth or other wine-based aperitifs. Was it in ancient Egypt, where wine was often flavored with honey and frankincense? Or was it in ancient Greece, with a crude form of retsina? Frankly, no one will ever know. However, it is much more enlightening to examine the developments of aperitifs in the course of more recent centuries.

As early as the sixteenth century, monastic communities throughout Europe were producing elixirs or spirits flavored by herbs and spices, which were offered to the poor and sick as tonics for good health and long life. These often had extremely strong alcohol levels (55–60 percent proof), and sometimes were not very palatable. This left a gap in the market for producers to try to make something more acceptable for popular consumption, based on the most easily available ingredients. Therefore, most bitters were created in northern Europe, where distillation was widespread, and most wine-based aperitifs in southern Europe's vineyard regions. If a local wine was poor, adding a selection of herbs and spices could substantially improve it. With fortification acting as a preservative, drinks were able to travel – consequently, the discovery of the New World added a number of important lucrative markets.

In France and Italy – the greatest rivals for aperitif production and consumption – the emergence of bars, cafés, and restaurants also provided a new marketplace for aperitifs. The competition with inns and alehouses encouraged these establishments to seek new drinks eagerly to gain customers. One of the first brands to be created during this market growth was Pernod. It was originally made around 1790 in Switzerland, but was not sold under any patented name until early in the nineteenth century, when the Pernod family purchased it from its second owner. Its arrival in Paris caused a sensation, as sipping aperitifs became fashionable, with brand names a topic of polite conversation.

An *alchemist laboratory*

Turin was the center for vermouth production in the nineteenth century

To the south of the Alps, Turin, the capital of Savoy, became the center for vermouth production. By the eighteenth century, Turin had grown into a thriving commercial center, where the arts, culture, and civilized society flourished. It is still possible to capture its atmosphere by visiting the ancient Teatro Carignano near the cathedral, and then slipping into the nearby Cambio Restaurant, whose decor remains unchanged since that time. Here the portly, young *maître licoriste* Gaspare Campari served aperitifs to King Vittorio Emmanuele II and his Prime Minister, Cavour. A *maître licoriste* was a master drink maker, who learned the properties and characteristics of numerous herbs and spices, and knew how to mix original drinks from them. In fact, in the 1840s, the founders of two of the most important aperitif dynasties, Gaspare Campari and Alessandro Martini, were both apprentice *maître licoristes* at the Bass bar in Turin. In those days, each major café-bar boasted its own *maître licoriste*, who jealously guarded the secret recipe for the most successful house *aperitivo*. This café-bar trade eventually developed into a giant industry, with the names of Italy, Turin, or Milan and their brands being displayed in bars throughout the world.

Gaspare Campari later left Savoy, and eventually moved to Milan. Although there was no interest in his vermouth, his bitters became a legend. Alessandro Martini, on the other hand, remained in Savoy, where he was to see his name become synonymous with vermouth all over the world.

VERMOUTH

Vermouth is the most widely known aperitif, with Cinzano and Martini being the strongest international brand names. The first branded vermouth was Carpano at Turin in 1786. This tiny house produced a sweet red style, which soon became fashionable. Trade quickly spread over the border to southern France, bringing a speedy response from Joseph Noilly, a wine producer in the ancient Mediterranean port of Marseillan.

An old Martini production line

In 1800, he introduced the first French dry vermouth.

However, the true home of Vermouth was still the ancient kingdom of Savoy. It occupied most of today's north-west Italy, and various tracts of southern and eastern France. Savoy had extensive vineyards, which, due to the growers' lack of expertise, produced inferior wines, largely lacking in character – a criticism that could not be applied to many wines from comparable vineyards today.

Herbs and spices from all over the world are used in the production of vermouth

At that time in France, Spain, and Portugal, wine-growers were already selling simple fortified wines, but in Savoy, most wines did not possess enough flavor to succeed on their own. Therefore, bartenders and wine producers added mixtures of herbs and spices that they devised themselves. Most reference works insist, strangely, that vermouth was originally only made with white wine, but some producers have been making Rosso, or Red Vermouth, with red wines since the early nineteenth century. Dry white vermouth followed a couple of generations later, with medium-dry Bianco in the 1960s and Rosé shortly after. Nowadays, however, virtually all Red vermouth is made from white wine blended with caramel to give it an amber hue.

The word "vermouth" derives from the Old-High-German word *vermud*, meaning wormwood (in Latin, *Artemisia absinthium*, from which the word *absinthe* arose), the name of a bitter-wood bark. It was known as wormwood because it was a successful "vermifuge," or agent for dispelling worms from the body. It was recommended by doctors and herbalists for that purpose, and was known for its expurgatory effect. As a medicine it was extremely bitter and unpleasant to take, but diluting it in wine flavored with various herbs and spices made a much-needed but otherwise repulsive

A selection of the herbs and spices that feature in Martini vermouth

beverage acceptable. Thus, out of medical needs, a delicious drink was born — and with it, the new practice of sipping, since previously most drinkers gulped their wine or beer.

Wormwood also played a part in anise-flavored aperitifs such as Pernod (see directory). Just as the monks had provided stronger alcoholic medicines for those who were feeble, many saw the development of vermouth as having a double advantage — first, for the good of one's health, and second, as a drink that was pleasing to the palate. These days, wormwood bark is no longer used, but the leaves and roots are ingredients in other aperitifs.

The Noilly Prat plant in the small fishing village of Marseillan

French vermouth is similar to its Italian competitor in many ways, but a major difference can be seen by the thousands of annual visitors to the cellars of Noilly Prat, the name that is synonymous with it. There, after fortification, it is placed in oak barrels and aged outdoors for two years. Consequently, its maturation is influenced by all the variations of temperature, atmosphere, and weather. Centuries ago, local growers discovered that aging fortified wines was substantially accelerated when left in such conditions. Some people in the South of France refer to this style as a *vin cuit*, or cooked wine.

The Savoy vermouth tradition stretched as far north as Chambery, and when the kingdom was later divided between Italy and France, the Chambery vermouths became French. In effect, their use of local wines and herbs led to a slightly different, lighter style than Italian vermouths, reflected today by the Dolin and Gaudin brands.

AROMATIZED WINES

In Paris in the 1840s, something very different was happening. The French government was helping to create two famous wine-based aperitifs; Dubonnet and St. Raphaël. France's colonies in North Africa paid a great price in human lives, as men died by the thousands from malaria. A bitter-wood bark from the cinchona tree, quinine, was known to protect against malaria, but was extremely unpalatable to swallow. Therefore, the French government announced that it would award bursaries to anyone who could create successful, wine-based recipes to facilitate its consumption. Two men, Joseph Dubonnet and Alphonse Juppet, responded. They both succeeded after prolonged, thorough research, but apparently at considerable cost – in Dubonnet's case, to his marriage, and in Juppet's, to his health. They both created drinks fortified with brandy, flavored with aromatic herbs, and aged for around two years, which proved so popular in North Africa (sold under the name Quinquina) that they were distributed in mainland France, where they achieved instant success.

The surrender of Abd-el-Kader

18

These aromatized wines were produced in both white and red varieties, and were initially drunk straight. Over a period of time, with experimentation, further additions were made. Soon, ice and a slice of lemon or sometimes orange, were added, and later, in the twentieth century, a fashion arose for lengthening aromatized wines with tonic or soda water, bitter lemon, and lemonade. In Europe, after the Second World War, the red variety achieved great popularity, while the white eventually disappeared, and the word *quinquina* or quinine was removed from the labels.

In the meantime, the production of Dubonnet in the U.S. was undergoing a curious transformation. The Schenley company (best known for American whiskey) were the appointed Dubonnet agents, but under a special arrangement, they were allowed to make to the blending of the aperitif to suit their market needs, which Schenley

A St. Raphaël poster showing the drink's creator, Alphonse Juppet, and the eponymous saint

considered to be different from those in Europe. The result was a variation of the brand, including differences in bottling and labelling, that was sold in the U.S.. Today, Dubonnet in the U.S. is marketed by another American whiskey company, Heaven Hill, who produce it under licence in California. They have returned to Joseph Dubonnet's original recipe, and have repackaged the bottles in a more traditional style to reflect the drink's French heritage.

FORTIFIED WINES

All the following fortified wines are the result of white or red wines having been made in the normal manner, then fortified by adding young, purified brandy. No herbs or spices are used.

Sherry

Sherry is the most widely known aperitif among fortified wines. Its unique characteristics are the result of several key factors that influence its production in the Jerez region in southern Spain.

The first is the chalky-white *albariza* soil, which is extremely deep, and allows the roots of the vines to penetrate to a level where they can find water and nourishment in what must be one of the hottest, driest climates in Europe.

Another factor is the mysterious *flor* which settles on the surface of Fino and Manzanilla styles when they begin aging in wood. *Flor* is a yeast that occurs in very few locations around the world. Even within the same *bodegas* (above-ground cellars) it will only settle on certain sherries, indicating to the producer that the particular wine will develop into a *fino*, that is, the driest style of sherry. The same criterion applies in the area of Sanlucar de Barrameda, also within the Jerez region, where the term *manzanilla*

Tio Pepe sherry's first sample room

is used instead of fino, to describe its distinguishing characteristic of a slightly salty flavor. When *flor* does not develop on the surface of a sherry, it indicates that it will be an *oloroso*. In fundamental terms, only the two sherry varieties of fino and oloroso exist. Others, such as amontillado and pale cream, are created by blending finos and/or olorosos, and often by adding permitted wines for sweetening.

Flor, the yeast layer that develops in fino sherries

A third factor is the solera system, which both ages and blends the sherries. Long rows of sherry butts (barrels) are stacked four levels high. Wine for bottling is always taken from the butts at ground level. It is then replaced by sherry from the row above, and that replenished with sherry from the third row, then the third row with wine from the top level, which itself is partially restocked with new wine.

Sherry has existed since ancient times, with the vineyards having been initially planted by Greek settlers in the fifth century B.C. Later, Spain was occupied by the Moors, and Jerez became a frontier city. Inhabitants of Christendom on one side of the frontier wall could enjoy the local wine, but residents on the other side had to conform to the Muslim ban on alcohol. From this situation arose the city's full name, Jerez de la Frontera.

Malaga

Directly south of Montilla-Moriles, and just east of Gibraltar, where the Mediterranean Sea begins, lies Malaga, where fortified wine production is an ancient practice. The solera method is similarly employed, and the grape varieties used are Moscatel and Pedro Ximenez. The Malaga-Lagrima style and old Solera Malaga are very appealing. Lagrima is made only from the free-running grape juice that bursts forth from the weight of the ripest grapes.

Madeira

Not all Madeira wine can claim the description of aperitif. Sercial, the driest style, Verdelho, a medium-dry (both named after their respective grape varieties), and Rainwater, another medium-dry, are all ideal chilled, or kept cool in the cellar as aperitifs.

Vineyards were first planted on the old, volcanic island of Madeira early in the fifteenth century. When later, in the sixteenth century, merchants began shipping Madeira to various countries, it was not fortified, and was always shipped in casks, usually being sold under the name of the grape variety – Malvasia, Malmsey, or Terrantez.

Shipping came to an abrupt halt when the Spanish occupied the island from 1580 to 1665. It was probably during this period that the solera system, as used in sherry production, was introduced, and the first fortification took place.

Madeira attracted wine producers of various nationalities, and their different requirements saw a range of styles develop. Some shippers began specializing in "vintage Madeira" by dating wines from outstanding years. Also, a unique aging process was introduced, called *estufagem*. This was an aging cellar in a roof space, where the Madeira was exposed to daily fluctuations in temperature and weather. Nowadays, this method has been replaced by artificially creating extremes in temperatures in a special cellar.

Blandy's Lodge

Port

Port is a fortified wine from grapes grown in the Douro valley of northern Portugal. It is traditionally aged in stone lodges 65 miles downstream in Vila Nova de Gaia, which is a suburb of the city of Oporto. It is mostly sold through old shipping companies, known as "port houses," which are mainly of British, Portuguese, and Dutch origin.

Harvesting into traditional baskets

For around three centuries, the tawny style was perceived as an aperitif, but in 1934, Taylor's, one of the most prestigious houses, began marketing the first white port. Since then, many other brands have followed suit. White port is made from white grapes, and all other ports are pressed from red grapes. Also, when the grapes are crushed for white port, the skins are usually removed quickly in order to keep a clean, healthy color. White port is generally aged little, while all the other ports are matured in oak for long periods.

Port vineyards in the Douro Valley

Marsala

Marsala comes from the regulated DOC vineyard region of that name surrounding the ancient city of Marsala, on the west coast of the island of Sicily, in Italy. It is a fortified wine that can be either *oro* (gold) or red and is sometimes, but not always, made using the solera system. Marsala is produced by blending local wines with a *mistelle* and cooking must.

The Florio cellars at Marsala

A *mistelle* is made by adding neutral grape alcohol to freshly pressed grape juice. This prevents the grape juice from fermenting and retains all the natural sweetness of the grape sugar. Cooking must is made by concentrating and heating fresh grape juice until its sugars caramelize. The end product is a rich, sticky syrup.

Marsala is drunk both as an aperitif and as a dessert wine.

Vins Doux Naturels

A small number of fortified wines from southern France are often drunk as aperitifs, but these do not involve muscat grapes. These *Vins Doux Naturels* (naturally sweet wines that are fortified) are often based on the full-bodied Grenache grape variety, with generic names like Banyuls, Maury, Rasteau, and Rivesaltes being displayed on blackboards during summer months to tempt tourists to sample them. Their bottles usually identify that they have been aged for five or ten years.

One of the most unusual of these is Maury, which has its own *appellation contrôlée* region in the foothills of the Pyrenees. It is a *vin cuit*, which is aged outdoors for 12 months, for the very same reason as Noilly Prat. Maury is placed in large, glass demi-johns that stand within a netted area to protect them from birds, with the necks unceremoniously covered in old soup cans to prevent insects from taking an unexpected bath.

Maury aged outdoors in glass demi-johns

MUSCATS

For the sake of this book, muscats have been separated from *French Vins Doux Naturels*, although technically, most French muscats fall within the official category of *Vins Doux Naturels* in their own country. Generally, in the northern hemisphere, muscats are drunk both as aperitifs and dessert wines, while in the southern hemisphere, they tend to be made in a heavier style that is more suited to accompanying desserts.

The dominant grape variety used for producing muscat wines is the muscat of Alexandria, which is a sweet, aromatic grape with numerous cousins. When left on the vine for late ripening, the muscat grape provides a rich, golden juice that produces some of the most fragrant and delicious wines. These are usually found in Mediterranean climates, and excel from east to west.

The muscat of Samos has been a Greek delicacy since time immemorial. Other examples are Moscatel de Setubal in Portugal, and the various French muscats. Of the latter, Muscat de Beaumes-de-Venise and Muscat-de-Rivesaltes are most widely known and are found in many international markets.

Vineyard at the foot of the Canigou, France

BITTERS

There can be little doubt that easy access to suitable ingredients encouraged the earliest tradition of any of these classic aperitifs. In the Netherlands, the production of bitters using corn spirit as a base began as early as the sixteenth century, with companies like Lucas Bols in Amsterdam being founded in 1575. Interestingly, nearly three centuries later, when Gaspare Campari first sold his

Gaspare Campari

classic aperitivo in Milan, he identified his recipe as *Bitter all'uso d'Hollanda* (bitters in the Dutch fashion). Indeed, legend has it that the term "cocktail" originates from that same period, when the early Dutch settlers in America were said to have used quills plucked from a cock's tail feathers to paint infected tonsils with a form of homemade, alcoholic bitters.

Over a period of time, other bitters emerged, sometimes of quite different character. Among the more unusual is Cynar, the Italian artichoke-flavored *aperitivo*. In some European countries it is virtually impossible to find, but in Italy and some other parts of southern Europe, and within Italian-American communities in the United States, it is so successful that its worldwide sales of around 12 million bottles make it the fifth largest-selling bitters.

By contrast, the unique, Trinidad-based, Angostura bitters was originally created by Dr. J.G.B. Siegert in Venezuela in 1824. Since then, it has played a key role as an ingredient in other aperitifs, cocktails, and even culinary dishes, but although it can be found in many bars around the world in its small, distinctive, paper-wrapped bottle, it has never attracted popularity as a drink on its own. Its owners have attempted to convince bartenders that it should be sold in larger volume, mixed with tonic water and ice,

An illustration from the first Campari publicity brochure

but the suggestion has not succeeded. Yet who can deny that it plays its part as an aperitif?

The recipes for all the various, branded bitters appear to be the most closely guarded secrets of all. Campari has a system whereby the company president is the only person who knows the entire formula, and one morning a week he personally produces the concentrate with the help of eight employees, each of whom knows only a few of the 68 herbs, spices, and wood barks involved. The door to the herb-and-spice room has a notice warning that any unauthorised employee found inside there faces instant dismissal. The reason for the secrecy is clear – there have been numerous attempts to counterfeit most major bitters, but fortunately, no one has yet been able to balance a recipe correctly.

Most of the recipes are prepared in the form of concentrates that require dilution. This is usually achieved by blending them with purified water, neutral or other suitable alcohol, and a sugar solution.

Artichoke extract gives Cynar its distinctive flavor

PASTIS

Like bitters, this category dominates the aperitif market in some countries, yet finds little popularity in others. Originally, the vast majority of these drinks were aniseed-flavored, with an extremely long tradition stretching back to around 1,600 BC, when they were mentioned in the Papyrus of Ebers. However, this was over 3,000 years before such drinks were produced using a spirit base, and so they bore only a limited resemblance to the pastis of today. Aniseed was a great favorite, both among the Greeks in Asia Minor and the Moors, who brought it to southern Europe when they occupied parts of Italy and the Iberian peninsula in the eighth century AD. They utilized it as a cleansing agent for flavoring unclean water to make it harmless to the digestive system.

The classic French tradition for pastis began in the Valais region of Switzerland following the French Revolution in 1789. A French scientist created a new aperitif called *absinthe* based on two

French revolution crowd surges toward the Hotel de Ville after the murder of the Bastille governor

main ingredients – wormwood bark (Latin *Artemisia absinthium*), and the roots of the giant *star anis* plant that grew in the western Alps of Switzerland and France.

A generation later, the Pernod family transferred the production of the drink to Pontarlier, in France, where both main ingredients were readily available. Subsequently, Pontarlier became the home of classic French pastis, with several brands coming to prominence in the late nineteenth century, including Terminus, which was made famous by the celebrated Tamagno-designed poster.

In the last two decades of the nineteenth century, absinthe became the most fashionable aperitif in Paris, and it was popularized by Henri de Toulouse-Lautrec in his painting, *The Absinthe Drinkers*, as well as by certain authors. Wild stories also emerged about its aphrodisiac effect. Early in the twentieth century, medical research blamed absinthe for the permanent mental illnesses suffered by many heavy drinkers, identifying its toxic properties specifically with the actual Artemisia absinthium bark. As a result,

Star anise

some governments banned the drink, including the French in 1915. This left the drinks producers hastily seeking for suitable alternative ingredients. The Pernod company carried out lengthy research, and found it was possible to use the leaves and roots of the same plant without any risks, and so created their new recipe, which was launched as *Pernod Anise* in 1926. It was an aperitif that looked like absinthe, but had a new, distinctive taste that lacked the original bitterness. Naturally, consumers were suspicious, and sought names they could trust, a philosophy that led to Pernod becoming a major brand very quickly, with a host of other houses trying to imitate it. These imitations became known as the *pastiche* drinks therefore, and the word simply became adapted to pastis.

Pastis Variations

In Marseilles, a separate pastis tradition evolved of flavoring drinks with licorice, which purported to have a similar cleansing effect to aniseed, and also a settling, digestive effect. It remained of local interest until 1932, when Paul Ricard launched his pastis throughout France. Today, it is by far the largest-selling of all pastis, at nearly 90 million bottles per annum.

Aniseed

In Bordeaux, a third tradition emerged in 1755, when Marie Brizard founded her company. She had been a philanthropist who provided a clinic for the sick and the poor. On one occasion, a grateful patient gave her a recipe for a medicinal drink based on aniseed, which she adapted for commercial use. It quickly found favor, enjoying a heyday in the nineteenth century. Nowadays, its popularity has diminished, and the company is best known for its range of classic liqueurs.

Spain has also contributed both *anis* and *chinchon* to the development of pastis, but for some reason, these have never had much widespread success outside the Spanish-speaking world.

In the Greek world, ouzo is a great favorite, and is responsible for many a holiday hangover. It is derived from the aniseed-based drinks that were first known in pre-Christian days. These were often blended with resin, and were considered to have good digestive properties. Nowadays, ouzo is widely produced both in Greece and Cyprus, and is greatly appreciated by their populations. A similar pastis called Raki is found in Turkey.

Marie Brizard

OTHER APERITIFS

Montilla

About 100 miles inland and northeast of Jerez de la Frontera lies the region of Montilla-Moriles. The local wine is known as *Montilla*, and it is quite similar to sherry, but is surprisingly unfortified. Again, it is blended and aged using the solera system, and *flor* arrives on the surface of many wines. Its 15 percent alcohol-by-volume strength is achieved through natural fermentation. The blend of grapes also varies, as the Palomino is not grown, and the Pedro Ximenez variety, which in Jerez provides a sweetening wine, supplies 90 percent of the wine in Montilla, covering all styles from dry to sweet.

Pedro Ximenez grapes are laid out on rush mats to dry in the sun

33

Pineau des Charentes

Pineau des Charentes is extremely popular with tourists in western France, and when served chilled, delights both dry and sweet palates. It can only be produced within the official Cognac region in France, and is made by adding young brandy to the grape must immediately after it has been crushed. This action prevents fermentation, and retains all the natural grape sugar.

Ratafia

In the Burgundy and Champagne regions there are two similar aperitifs that are produced in very small quantities, and are known as *ratafia de Bourgogne* and *ratafia de Champagne*.

Crème de cassis

Some aperitifs do not sit easily in any category, such as *crème de cassis* (black currant liqueur) from Dijon in Burgundy. Although it is identified as a liqueur, it is renowned as a key ingredient in two aperitifs, Kir and Kir Royal, made by adding it to dry white wine or sparkling wine respectively. Its use as an aperitif is credited to Canon Felix Kir, a French resistance hero in the Second World War who served as the mayor of Dijon. He added crème de cassis to lesser-quality white wines, serving them to all his visitors.

Advocaat, Guignolet, Rinquinquin, and Archers

Advocaat from the Netherlands, which is made from brandy and eggs, is still drunk by many. *Guignolet*, the increasingly rare French cherry aperitif, is normally consumed on ice, and has few competitors. *Rinquinquin* and *Archers* are two quite different peach-flavored aperitifs. The French Rinquinquin is made from peaches, herbs, and spices. Canadian Archers is a blend of peaches and neutral spirit.

ADVERTISING AND PUBLICITY

ART AND APERITIFS

As with many drinks, early advertising was chiefly through posters, some of which became classic editions that even today are still sought after by collectors – for example, the late-nineteenth-century Tamagno poster for Terminus Absinthe. In the early twentieth century, this art form was to reach new heights through the encouragement of Davide Campari, the son of the company's founder, and the man who really built the brand. He was a great patron of the arts in Milan, and personally commissioned many notable posters. He also commissioned a portrait of the beautiful opera singer, Lina Cavalieri, with whom he was in

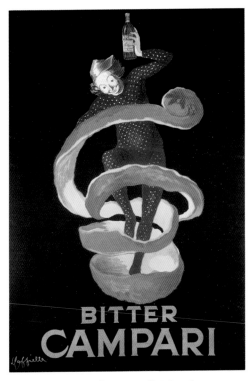

Campari's famous "Folletto" poster

A Martini poster

love; the portrait was famously reproduced on an ashtray, and was one of the company's most memorable advertisements.

Campari's policy was to allow poster designers artistic freedom, providing their work met three basic criteria: they must clearly display the brand name; use uncomplicated colors; and the brand should be incorporated naturally in the picture. Among the most memorable posters are Cappiello's "Folletto" (1921), which displayed a dancing clown in a spiral of orange peel, holding a Campari bottle high above his head, and Enrico Sacchetti's "Viveur," depicting a man in top hat and tails. The company continued the practice in 1958 with Rolli's seaside poster, and in the 1960s with Stroppa's "Elephant."

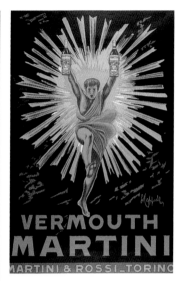

A Martini poster

Another famous poster, known as "The Don," proved immensely versatile. It was sold to Sandeman, the port and sherry house, by an anonymous salesman in September 1928. It shows the shadowy silhouette of a man wearing a sombrero, said to represent sherry, and a Portuguese student's cloak, to denote port. At the time, it was the vogue to use French posters, but the artist concerned was a struggling Scot named George Massiot Brown. He colluded with the salesman to pretend that he was French, abbreviated George to the initial G, suggested that Massiot should be pronounced with a French accent, and dispensed with Brown, completing the charade by signing the poster G. Massiot. The figure in the poster bore a similarity to the screen character known as "Zorro," and it was later discovered that the artist, who was a dedicated movie buff, had created the work in the same week that "The Gaucho," the third of the Zorro films, premiered in London.

Sandeman's "Don"

Sandeman bought the poster for 50 guineas ($87.40) and had two versions printed. In the first, the figure held a sherry glass containing straw-colored sherry, and in the second, the figure held a glass full of rich, red port. Three years later, Royal Doulton produced

"Viveur", one of Campari's best known posters

porcelain figures of the Don. In 1933, the poster was reprinted as the world's largest of its kind, measuring 130 x 29.25 feet. "The Don" was adopted by Sandeman as its logo, and a giant cut-out of the sherry version could be seen just outside Jerez de la Frontera, and a similar, port-drinking Don on the outskirts of Porto. Other sherry houses have used logos for many years, although some have devised their own, such as Gonzalez Byass, who displayed a flamenco guitarist, and Williams & Humbert, who have used "The Sherry Girl" as their trademark since the year 1939.

Recognition for the most imaginative aperitif advertising must surely go to John Harvey & Sons, noted for their Bristol Cream Sherry advertising. In 1912, they published an advertisement whose main claim read "sherry is the only wine which can be appreciated while smoking."

THE GREAT EXHIBITIONS

The arrival of the steam engine in the nineteenth century brought about a transformation in travel, and stimulated the desire to learn about other countries and their produce. Many traders and consumers were prepared to experiment with foreign goods of all kinds, including food and drink, but they wanted to be able to recognize trusted labels. This brand growth led to a fashion for great exhibitions, which attracted producers, merchants, and the wealthy alike.

Exhibitions were held in many of the world's great cities, including Moscow, Vienna, Brussels, Paris, London, Philadelphia, St Louis, Buenos Aires, and Sydney. One of the highlights of these occasions were the international competitions, where medals and diplomas were awarded in various categories. Wine and drink brands often reproduced them on the labels. Until its

Diploma awarded to Amer Picon at the Strasbourg Colonial Exhibition

An award certificate received by Martini

1997 re-packaging, Martini Vermouth boasted 40 medals at the top of its label and displayed 6 of them. Scholtz Hermanos Malaga Solera 1885 displays ten medals on its label, plus the announcement of its Diploma of Honor at Antwerp in the very same year.

TV COMMERCIALS

Television commercials provided a new opportunity to reach the general public in its millions and this tempted the drinks companies to consider whether or not international advertisements could be made that would have universal appeal. These were not often successful because of language and cultural problems. However, the classic, black-and-white Dubonnet commercials of the 1960s starring the great French comedian, Fernandel, attracted widespread acclaim.

In recent years, international budgeting has been minimized, with funds being invested country by country. Advertising of all kinds has now become so expensive that many brands are reluctant to spend heavily, instead preferring to discount special offers or to tempt consumers with valuable promotions.

SERVING APERITIFS

GLASSWARE

The choice of glassware can be remarkably diverse, as once aperitifs were bottled, rather than made to order on the spot, the style of glass used was largely influenced by local tradition and its practicality.

There is no one "correct" glass for vermouth, because this depends on how it is being served. In the U.S., vermouth is usually served in a narrow tumbler, while in Italy and France, a short-stemmed wine glass is preferred, with the vermouth served on ice with a slice of lemon.

Some customers insist on having Martini vermouth served in a Martini glass, but not many people know that the Martini glass was designed to hold a Martini cocktail, which is not at all related to the vermouth of the same name. The Martini cocktail was created by and named after a New York-based Hispanic bartender, called Martinez, in 1911. It comprised two parts gin and two parts Noilly Prat, because at that time, Noilly was the only dry vermouth available in international markets, and Martini & Rossi had not yet introduced their Dry Vermouth. Martinez simply wanted it to appeal to the city's numerous Italian-owned bars, and so adapted his name to Martini.

Martini cocktail

Campari offers five basic suggestions for serving its bitters: on ice with a slice of orange; tall with soda and ice; *Camparino*, which is also tall with soda, but served from a pressure gun that delivers soda-water ready chilled; with orange juice and ice; and *shakerato*. As these five styles call for five different glasses, the company has never been able to identify with one individual glass design. Nevertheless, in the 1960s, an Italian designer was commissioned to create a stylish set of Campari glasses, which were favorably received when launched. However, although they looked wonderful, they proved to be

impractical and fragile, and were quickly withdrawn. More recently, Campari has introduced a new range of glasses, which have been favorably received.

Sherry makers, on the other hand, are almost unanimous in electing the *copita*, a slim, elegant, short-stemmed glass that tapers inwards at the top. The *copita* should usually be slightly less than half-full, allowing the drinker to swirl the sherry around the glass and savor the bouquet. Williams & Humbert are one of the few exceptions, as they prefer to recommend a tulip-shaped glass.

Copitas with oloroso, amontillado and fino sherry

APPETIZERS AND SNACKS

Aperitifs are as much appreciated at home as in bars and restaurants, and many of us have our own favorite snacks to accompany a pre-lunch drink. These serve several purposes – to prevent drinking alcohol on an empty stomach, which is not good for digestion; to start the meal-time process; and, of course, to go out and socialize.

The phrase "snacks and appetizers" is carefully chosen, as aperitifs are intended for consumption before food, and not with food. It is really only sherry drinkers in Spain who take their consumption of *fino* into the often extensive first course of *tapas*, and sometimes into the main course, especially when it is shellfish. Tapas are legendary and quite delicious, but they are not really an accompaniment to aperitifs – more like a substantial first course, with small plates containing everything from Serrano ham to ink squid and jumbo shrimp, often presented with a tempting array of Spanish queen olives.

A *tempting array of tapas*

In neighboring Portugal, where white port is among the favorite aperitifs, snacks can be a small assortment of roasted almonds, olives, cherry tomatoes, and small cubes of smoked ham.

In Italy, customs vary depending on the region, but in a classic Turin café-bar, small dishes of nuts, olives, small savory crackers, potato chips, and bread sticks are served.

In the charming, white-washed coffee shops of Cyprus, green and black olives may be accompanied by green, un-ripe cherries and lemons, both served with salt and small portions of feta cheese. Villagers often sip ouzo as they snack, and then drink half a bottle of cheap brandy with the various main courses.

The finest French restaurants offer *amuse-gueules* or tastebud tempters – usually warm, mouth-watering savories, whose purpose is to whet the appetite in anticipation of the full meal.

By contrast, in parts of Provence, a large dish of raw vegetables is placed on the table. The colors alone are tempting, with the purple hues of eggplants, red, yellow, and green bell peppers, and the complementary shades of artichokes and onions. These are often accompanied by various dips that are carefully chosen so as not to overpower the aperitifs. Also, especially with pastis, an assortment of dried fruits and nuts may be served.

Metzes are favorite snacks in Cyprus and Greece

The wisest choice is to keep appetizers simple, and to avoid strong-flavored items that will overpower the palate – leave those for the main courses, which can be balanced with suitable wines.

Olives and raw vegetables are often served in Provence

APERITIF RITUALS OF CLASSIC BARS AROUND THE WORLD

With the expansion of cities in the seventeenth and eighteenth centuries, bars proliferated, and as they diversified, naturally appealed to a different clientele. The search for the highest standards led to the emergence of the classic café-bars in Turin, Milan, and elsewhere, which offered an attractive alternative for consuming aperitifs. The prosperous would often meet there by appointment, enjoy a vermouth or bitters, and then stroll a short distance to dine in a suitable restaurant.

The Campari bar in Milan's Galleria

In Paris and other major French cities, aperitifs are usually served in brasseries and in good restaurants. Service in brasseries is almost always rapid, but presentation varies considerably. In good restaurants, "Vous désirez un aperitif?" is normally the waiter's first question, and it is always fascinating to watch his reaction to the order. A curt nod might follow a demand for a whiskey, a slight smile may be permitted for a glass of champagne, but for the foreigner who demands a pastis, a "bien sûr" and sweep of the hand is guaranteed. In seconds, a classic, triangular-shaped Ricard water bottle is transferred from the refrigerator to the table, and with it, the distinctive, narrow, slightly fluted pastis glass.

The triangular-shaped Ricard bottle

He then waits to see if you are a traditionalist, who will take it – correctly – one part pastis and five parts water, or whether you will follow the nouveaux riches and order ice. The higher the marks the waiter awards you, the better the service for the rest of the meal!

In Giannino's classic bar in the center of Milan, you are likely to find the bartender wearing spotlessly white gloves, as he seldom touches anything with his hands apart from opening bottles. The head waiter will then lead you to a table, where another waiter takes your order to the bartender, who carefully pours the drinks, always one at a time, to avoid error. He uses tongs, scissors, and a knife to transform olives, slices of lemon or orange, and the orange peel into remarkable garnishes. He then pours each drink into an assortment of stylish, perfectly clean glasses. The tall glasses for bitters lengthened with soda will always be frosted.

Today the diversity of bars is quite astonishing, but the top premises still have that aura that is best demonstrated by the excellence of their service. In the legendary Harry's Bar in Venice, great care is taken to make all the guests feel comfortable, with small, exquisitely presented selections of appetizers placed before each one and assistance offered. The olives are the finest, the lemon peel has that green tinge that assures sufficient acidity, and the limes are just perfect. Famous bars cannot afford to lose their

Harry's Bar in Venice

reputations; their golden rule is that classic must remain classic, and if Ernest Hemingway enjoyed his Martini there with the finest green olives, then you should expect the same!

In the U.S., the stylish Hunt Club at Darien, Connecticut, is a perfect place to observe a Campari Soda served *properly*. The bartender takes a tall slim tumbler, pours a generous measure of the colorful red bitters, adds some ice, then seizes a soda gun attached to a long pipe. He pulls the trigger from around three feet away, lengthening the drink amidst the most elegant froth. Then he places it on the bar for all to observe. If on the other hand one requests a Campari on ice, you can be certain of the correct garnish, a slice of orange and not that mistaken wedge of lemon that clashes with the drink's bitter-sweet taste.

The legendary Norman at the bar in the Ritz-Carlton Hotel on the south side of New York's Central Park needs to meet you once only. He will introduce himself, ask your name and if you would care for an aperitif. Whether you order a Martini Extra-Dry, a Noilly Prat or a Pernod the video camera inside his brain will register your name and your choice and when you return, even if it is 12 months later, he will acknowledge your name and ask if you would care for the same drink.

London is these days better-known for its trendy night-clubs than its classic bars. Most of the latter are found in the luxury hotels. It can be a charming experience to visit the Dorchester, Claridges or the Ritz and sit in the bar sipping an aperitif while a pianist plays in the background. You should buy a little style with your aperitif, for that is what it offers you.

Harry's Bar, Venice, in 1933

PART TWO

THE BRANDED
DIRECTORY

THE APERITIF DIRECTORIES

The aperitif is a drink synonymous with style and elegance. Its prime role is neither to quench the thirst, nor to accompany food but to tempt partakers to relax and converse before dining.

Aperitifs are complex drinks, with often closely guarded, secret recipes, and histories as fascinating as any novel. In the two directories – Branded and Generic – which comprise the second part of this book, you will find a vast array of drinks. Some are household names; others are more obscure but no less interesting. The Branded Directory features aperitifs that are generally identified by their individual brand names, and includes a large range of labels, such as the world-renowned brands of Campari or Dubonnet, and also brands like Cocchi Barolo Chinato, which has a rich history, but a far smaller distribution.

The aperitifs in the Generic Directory are those normally referred to in conversation by their generic names. The terms "sherry," "Madeira," and "port" are commonly used, and consumers are likely to ask for an amontillado sherry or a glass of muscat, rather than an individual brand. To illustrate this section further, various prominent labels have been included and are used as examples.

A glossary of some of the more technical terms used in the book is given below.

GLOSSARY

albariza A unique, chalky white soil found in southern Spain.

aldehydes Unstable substances created by the oxidation of alcohol.

arrope A Spanish word for syrup produced from heating grape must, referred to elsewhere as cooking must. Although used primarily for sweetening, it also adds color.

barcos rabelos Ancient, high-tillered, wooden boats previously used for shipping port down the River Douro.

bodegas Spanish for above-ground cellars.

canteiros A Portuguese word denoting the area where some Madeiras are aged in casks placed in racks within the eaves of the cellar buildings.

copita A slim, elegant tulip-shaped glass.

esthers Invisible chemical components found in wines and drinks that influence their bouquet.

estufagem A heating chamber used in the production of Madeira, which treats the wine over a short period by raising and lowering its temperature. It is the modern successor to *canteiros*.

flor A mysterious, wild, yeast-like substance that appears on the surface of new *fino* sherries and a few other fortified wines. It is most widely found in southern Spain.

fortified wine Generic term used for all wines that have been fortified with alcohol to add strength and stability.

infusion The process of soaking herbs and spices in hot water to extract their flavors.

lagar A stone tank, often built of granite, used in Portugal to tread grapes.

lees The solid matter left after the fermentation of a wine. Some wines are allowed to age on their lees for maximum flavor.

maceration The soaking of herbs and spices in alcohol to extract their flavors.

mistelle or mistella Made by adding alcohol to fresh grape juice before it commences fermentation. This action retains the freshest fruit flavors and the natural grape sugars. *Mistelles* are often used in the blending of various aperitifs to add structure and natural sweetness.

must Freshly-crushed grape juice during its fermentation.

neutral alcohol Young spirit distilled from various organic material. It is colorless and flavorless.

pipe A barrel of between 145-155 gallons (500-550 liters). It originates from the Portuguese *pipas* tree.

quinta A Portuguese term for farm.

ruby A rich, red port in its youth.

sack From the Spanish word *sacar*, meaning to ship, or to go out.

schnapps A German word used to describe fruit-based white spirits.

solera A traditional barrel system found mostly in Spain, where the casks are usually placed four rows high. It both blends and ages wines. The oldest wine is at ground level, and after much of it is drawn for bottling, its casks are replenished with wine from the third row. The third row is then refilled from the second, and the second from the top. The wine of the new vintage is then added to the top row.

tawny A blended port of a lighter style than ruby. There are two styles of tawnies; the first are the relatively young, inexpensive wines that have been produced by blending ruby and white ports together; the second are the aged tawnies which began life as rubies but gradually became tawny-colored during the aging process.

tinajas Large terra cotta or concrete jars used to age wines in southern Spain.

vergine A Marsala to which no *mistelle* or cooking must has been added. In Spain, it sometimes describes a fortified wine that has been made from table wine and young brandy, with no additional flavorings.

vin cuit A wine that has been aged outdoors, either in barrels or large glass bottles.

vinous It indicates that a wine, or fortified wine, has a bouquet and flavor reminiscent of the grape variety used. Applied to a fortified wine, it suggests that the base wine is of good quality.

AMBASSADEUR

Something Different from Marseilles

Marseilles, an active center for production of pastis during the first half of the twentieth century, was also home to the aromatized wine, Ambassadeur. This was created by Eugène Pourchet in 1936 to compete with the two most popular quinine-based aperitifs of the period, Byrrh and St. Raphaël.

PRODUCTION

Ambassadeur is available in two styles, Blanc (white) and Rouge (red), but the former is far less available than the latter. The recipe for Ambassadeur Rouge includes many different herbs and spices, some of which are known – bitter peels from Bigerade oranges, sweet orange peels, vanilla, cocoa beans, and gentian flowers – not gentian roots, as used in many other aperitifs. Production is believed to involve macerating these

 KEY FACTS

COMPOSITION	A secret recipe of herbs and spices, which includes bitter- and sweet-orange peels, vanilla, cocoa, and gentian flowers, a mistelle, white or red wine (depending upon the style), and neutral alcohol
COUNTRY OF ORIGIN	France
WHERE PRODUCED	Thuir, France
PRIME MARKETS	France and Italy
VISITORS	Visitors are welcome. Tel: (33) 468530542

TO SERVE

Ambassadeur Blanc has a pale, golden color and a floral bouquet. It is quite elegant on the palate, with hints of sweetness and a distinctive, aromatic aftertaste.
It can be served as follows:

☆ *Well chilled, with a twist of lemon peel or a slice of orange*

☆ *Well chilled, and mixed 50/50 with gin*

Ambassadeur Rouge has a rich-ruby color and a delicate bouquet, with clear hints of raspberries, red currants, and cherries. It also has lingering notes of bitter and sweet oranges, which are confirmed on the palate.
It can be served:

☆ *Slightly chilled, with a twist of lemon peel or a slice of orange*

☆ *On ice, with a mixer of your choice*

ingredients in neutral alcohol and then blending the concentrate with white or red wines and a *mistelle*. The wines are first aged in large, oak casks before being flavored with the herbs. The purpose of this aging is to let the wines breathe and further develop their fruitiness.

Nowadays, Ambassadeur is owned by the Cusenier company, and is a sister brand to both Dubonnet and Byrrh. All three are produced in the same giant cellars at Thuir in the French Pyrenées.

The largest oak barrel in the world at Thuir

ANGOSTURA
AROMATIC BITTERS

A German Doctor in Venezuela

ngostura Aromatic Bitters was created in 1824 by a German doctor, J.G.B. Siegert, who was a surgeon in General Simón Bolivar's liberation army in Venezuela. Dr Siegert developed his recipe in the town of Angostura (later Ciudad Bolivar), situated on the Orinoco River, where he was posted as Surgeon General to the military hospital. Using aromatic herbs and spices that were available locally, he developed his elixir to combat the debilitating stomach and digestive disorders that so many of the soldiers suffered from at the time. He put his bitters on sale in 1830, and it became so popular in Venezuela that he set up a company to produce it. Upon his death in 1870, Dr Siegert's sons, Carlos and Alfredo, inherited the business, together with the secret formula for the drink. In 1875, they

KEY FACTS

COMPOSITION	*A secret recipe of herbs and spices, including gentian, and using a rum base*
COUNTRY OF ORIGIN	*Venezuela*
WHERE PRODUCED	*Trinidad*
PRIME MARKETS	*USA, Australia, UK*
AWARDS	*Royal Charter granted by Queen Elizabeth II of England*
VISITORS	*Visitors are welcome. Contact Mr. Glen Davis, telephone: (1-868) 6231841*

relocated the company to Trinidad, but it is still a family business to this day.

The quaint little (8.25 fluid ounces/230 ml) paper-wrapped bottle of Angostura Bitters is now found in bars, restaurants, and homes around the world. Angostura plays a role in hundreds of cocktails, yet it never takes the lead as a brand consumed in its own right, or as the principal ingredient in a drink. Nevertheless, it is a classic brand, enjoyed in millions of mixed drinks and cocktails that are drunk as aperitifs every day. It is also occasionally used as an ingredient in a number of cooking recipes.

PRODUCTION

Little is known about the actual recipe and production of Angostura, except that it is rum-based, with gentian being one of the most important of the 12 or so ingredients. Its dark-brown color is derived from completely natural vegetable coloring. The production process takes three months, and the resulting drink has a high abv of 44.7 percent for Europe and 45 percent for the USA.

TO SERVE

Not many people have ever drunk **Angostura Aromatic Bitters** on its own. It has an extremely aromatic bouquet, and a complicated, almost-medicinal palate, but it is rather too concentrated and bitter to be drunk alone. Angostura can be taken as a tall drink with chilled tonic or soda water, or used to give character to various cocktails, such as:

MANHATTAN
⅛ cup/40 ml whiskey
3 tsp/15 ml vermouth
2 dashes Angostura Bitters
Cherries to garnish
Stir the whiskey and vermouth together with ice, and strain into a cocktail glass. Decorate with cherries.

TRINIDAD
2 fluid ounces/50 ml rum
1 fluid ounce/25 ml lime juice
1 tsp/5 g confectioner's sugar
4 dashes Angostura Bitters
Place all ingredients into a cocktail shaker, and shake well. Pour into a cocktail glass over crushed ice and serve, garnished with a twist of lime peel.

APEROL

The Sociable Aperitif

Aperol was first made in 1919 by Barbieri, a small, family-owned company in Padua, near Venice, Italy. Silvio and Luigi Barbieri, sons of the company's founder, Giuseppe Barbieri, created the drink in response to the growing trend for aperitif consumption in France. Although production is now highly automated the process remains true to the original recipe. Hugely successful in Italy, where it claims 22 percent of its sector of the aperitif market, Aperol is only just beginning to build its export business. Aperol was one of the first brands to be advertised on television in Italy in the 1950s, and still makes wide use of the medium, with campaigns that focus on the fun and sociable aspects of the aperitif habit. In 1991, Aperol was bought by C. & C. International Ltd. in Dublin, Ireland, and later that

 KEY FACTS

COMPOSITION	Alcohol, water, orange essence, and various herbs
COUNTRY OF ORIGIN	Italy
WHERE PRODUCED	Canale in Northern Italy
WORLDWIDE ANNUAL SALES VOLUME	4,200,000 bottles
PRIME MARKETS	Italy, Germany, Malta
VISITORS	By appointment only, through Aperol's London-based public relations company. Telephone Spreckley Pittham on: (44-171) 3889988

TO SERVE

Aperol's color is a vibrant, glowing, orangey-red. Bitter peels with undertones of herbs can be detected on the nose. It has a fruity, slightly bitter taste, and is best served as follows:

☆ With orange or grapefruit juice

☆ On ice

☆ On ice, with soda

☆ Chilled

Individual, single-serving bottles of Aperol Soda at 3 percent abv have been available in Italy since 1995.

year the company merged with Barbero, one of Italy's premier wine and spirits companies.

PRODUCTION

Aperol is a spirit-based aperitif with a relatively low abv (alcohol by volume) of 11 percent. Altogether, it has 16 ingredients, including china bark (quinquina), Chinese rhubarb, gentian, and orange essence. Most of the herbs come from the Piedmont region of northern Italy where it is produced by Barbero. The product is bottled immediately after blending, ready to be marketed.

BARBERO VERMOUTH

Following the Glorious Piedmontese Tradition

The independently owned Barbero company was founded in Canale, in the Piedmont region of Italy, in 1891. Its main production is vermouth, of which it makes 1.8 million bottles per annum, covering the three most-popular styles – the dry white *Secco*, the medium-sweet *Bianco*, and traditional *Rosso*. In total, the company uses some 40 different herbs and spices in its production. However, the number varies depending on the required styles

PRODUCTION

As with other vermouths, the production of Barbero requires various alpine plants and flowers, and additional exotic spices. These are first mixed, then macerated in white wine for around 60 days before the concentrate of extracts is blended with neutral alcohol, white wines from Puglia, Romagna, and Sicily, and a sugar solution.

 KEY FACTS

COMPOSITION	*A secret blend of herbs and spices, white wine, and neutral-grape brandy*
COUNTRY OF ORIGIN	*Italy*
WHERE PRODUCED	*Canale, Italy*
WORLDWIDE ANNUAL SALES VOLUME	*1.8 million bottles*
PRIME MARKETS	*UK, Denmark, and the Czech Republic*

Being a relatively small producer compared with vermouth giants like Martini and Cinzano, Barbero has smaller overheads and has been able to price its product extremely competitively. Subsequently, it is succeeding in some important export markets.

TO SERVE

Barbero Secco has a pale-gold color and an elegant bouquet, with readily detectable floral notes, especially of roses. It is dry and tangy on the palate, with a light, herby finish.

Barbero Bianco is light gold in color, with a slightly herby bouquet. It is medium-dry on the palate, with a fairly complex aftertaste.

Barbero Rosso has a rich-amber hue, and possesses quite an aromatic bouquet. It is quite sweet and full-bodied on the palate, with a pleasant, herby aftertaste. All three styles can be served as follows:

☆ Straight, well chilled, and with lemon peel in a wide-brimmed glass

☆ On ice, in a large, wide glass

☆ As a tall drink on ice, with a choice of mixer, and garnished with a slice of lemon

Suggested combinations: Secco and tonic, Bianco and bitter lemon, Rosso and American ginger ale

BERGER

The Marseilles Tradition

The Berger company was founded in Marseilles in 1923 by Marie-Louis Gassier and is today controlled by his son, Benjamin Gassier. In the 1930s, Berger introduced a slogan, which is still used today, that ran *"Midi–Sept Heures, l'Heure de Berger"* ("Noon–7 o'clock, the hour of Berger"), promoting the idea of enjoying the brand at any time from noon to early evening. It quickly became a catchphrase in France, and anyone found sipping a drink earlier than usual could simply claim that it was *l'Heure de Berger*.

Nowadays, the company is famous for its two pastis, Berger Pastis and Berger Blanc and is the market leader for white, anise-based drinks.

BERGER BLANC

Berger Blanc differs from the other pastis in that it contains an extremely low quantity of natural plant extracts – barely 0.01 percent. The resulting drink is white, not yellow-green as other pastis are.

 KEY FACTS

COMPOSITION	*Aniseed, neutral alcohol, limited natural plant extracts, sugar syrup, and water*
COUNTRY OF ORIGIN	*France*
WHERE PRODUCED	*Lieusaint, Seine et Marne, France*
PRIME MARKETS	*France, Spain*

TO SERVE

Berger Blanc is a completely clear drink, with a pure, fresh bouquet of anise. It is sweeter than yellow pastis and a little fuller in the body.

Berger Blanc is best served as follows:

☆ Chilled, with black-currant juice, cordial, or crème de cassis

☆ One part Berger Blanc, well chilled, to five parts chilled water. The addition of water turns Berger Blanc a cloudy white

☆ Tall, on ice, with a mixer of your choice

PRODUCTION

The anise plant is macerated in alcohol to obtain the required extract, which makes up nearly 30 percent of the blend. Then, neutral alcohol, water, sugar syrup, and natural plant extracts are added. Finally, the blend is filtered to give a clean, clear, end product.

Aniseed

BERGER PASTIS

Berger Pastis is a pastis in the Marseilles tradition which uses licorice as a prime ingredient. As with Ricard, Janot and other exponents of that tradition, extracts of herbs and spices make up two percent of its volume and give it the yellow color, typical of Marseilles-style pastis.

TO SERVE

Berger Pastis has a light-yellow opaque color when mixed with water. It evokes an aromatic nose with anise being predominant. Licorice is recognizable on the slightly sweet palate. Berger Pastis is best served as follows:

☆ Chilled with black currant juice, cordial, or crème de cassis

☆ One part Berger Pastis – well chilled – to 5 parts of chilled water

☆ Tall on ice with a mixer of your choice

PRODUCTION

The anise flavoring that makes up almost 30 percent of Berger's Pastis final blend is extracted by macerating the plant in alcohol. To this are added neutral alcohol, sugar syrup, natural plant extracts (including licorice), caramel, and water. The drink is then filtered before being bottled.

 KEY FACTS

COMPOSITION BERGER PASTIS	Aniseed, licorice, other herbs and spices, caramel, neutral alcohol, sugar syrup, and water
COUNTRY OF ORIGIN	France
WHERE PRODUCED	Lieusant, Seine et Marne, France
PRIME MARKETS	France, Spain

BYRRH

A Catalan Drink

Byrrh is a Catalan drink produced at Thuir, in the foothills of the French Pyrenées, alongside its sister aperitif, Dubonnet. It was created by Simon Violet and a pharmacist friend, who together concocted the recipe at Perpignan, near the Spanish border, in 1870. Both local herbs and imported spices were used to flavor red Roussillon wines and, by the end of the nineteenth century, its production was controlled by Violet Frères. Nowadays it is owned by the Pernod-Ricard group. It is aged over a two-year period in oak barrels, and the company claims to have "the largest oak barrel in the world, with a capacity of one million liters."

PRODUCTION

Byrrh is an aromatized wine, and as is common with such brands, the details of

  KEY FACTS

COMPOSITION	A secret recipe of herbs and spices, red wine, mistelle, and neutral alcohol
COUNTRY OF ORIGIN	France
WHERE PRODUCED	Thuir, France
WORLDWIDE ANNUAL SALES VOLUME	1,800,000 litres
PRIME MARKETS	France, Belgium, Spain, Italy
VISITORS	Visitors are welcome at Caves Byrrh, 6 Boulevard Violet, 66300 Thuir, France. Tel: (33) 468530542

TO SERVE

Byrrh has a deep-red color, and a bouquet that is redolent of flowers and peels. It is drier than expected on the palate, and leaves an attractive, herby aftertaste. Byrrh can be served as follows:

☆ On ice, with bitter lemon and a slice of lemon

☆ On ice, with a slice of lemon or orange. A tall, narrow glass is recommended, as this enhances the bouquet

☆ On ice, with tonic, soda water, or lemonade, and a slice of lemon or orange

its ancient recipe are a strictly guarded secret. Of its 18 ingredients, those known include quinquina, coffee, and bitter oranges. Other flavorings come from local plants and herbs, which have been macerated. The concentrate is then blended with red wine (mainly from the Carignan grape variety from the Roussillon region), and neutral alcohol. A *mistelle* is added to provide natural sweetness and body. Byrrh is then aged in oak for a period of two to three years to provide balance and maturity.

The Pernod-Ricard headquarters

CAMPARI

Young Gaspare's Legacy

Campari was named after Gaspare Campari, who was born in 1828 in the small town of Castelnuovo in the province of Lombardy, before Italy was unified. At the age of 14, he became an apprentice *maître licoriste* (master drink-maker) at the prestigious Bass bar in Turin. It was an era when all the elegant café-bars had their own *maîtres licoristes*, who concocted original recipes with wine or spirit bases blended with various herbs and spices. House recipes became closely guarded secrets, and occasionally resulted in small, commercial production. It was from this tradition that brands

 KEY FACTS

COMPOSITION	A blend of selected herbs and spices, including peels and barks, neutral alcohol, sugar, and purified water. The recipe is a carefully guarded secret. Campari Soda also includes soda in a premixed bottle
COUNTRY OF ORIGIN	Italy
WHERE MANUFACTURED	Italy, France, Germany, Brazil, and Argentina
WORLDWIDE ANNUAL SALES VOLUME	33.6 million bottles
PRIME MARKETS	Italy, Germany, France, Switzerland, The Netherlands, Belgium, Greece, Spain, and Japan
AWARDS	Numerous nineteenth-century medals, and the papal warrant of Pope Pius XI
VISITORS	By appointment only. Telephone Dr. Bramani: (39-2) 24950283

such as Campari, Cinzano, Martini & Rossi, and Punt e Mes emerged.

His apprenticeship completed, Gaspare Campari became the *maître licoriste* of the renowned Cambio restaurant. There he served the elite of Turin society, including King Vittorio Emmanuel and his prime minister, Cavour.

Gaspare left Turin following the tragic loss of his first wife and two children. Eventually,

The Campari bar in Milan's Galleria

he remarried and, after a short spell in Novara, in 1862 he settled in Milan, his second wife's home city. He ran a fairly humble café in front of Milan's historic cathedral, the Duomo. Italy was in the process of unification, and a magnificent arcade – to be called La *Galleria* – was planned near the Duomo. This brought a dramatic upturn in Gaspare's fortunes, as his premises stood right in the way of the proposed development. Wisely, he declined all offers of financial compensation and demanded his own terms – to be given the very first premises at the main entrance to the Galleria.

There, in the stylish new *Café-Patisserie Campari* in 1867, Gaspare's wife Letizia offered customers his new bitters, which, it is believed, he had spent many years trying to perfect. Apparently, since his arrival in Milan, he had carried out various experiments blending numerous herbs and spices, before eventually finalizing his unique recipe.

In 1867, Davide Campari, Gaspare's youngest son, was the first child to be born in the Galleria, and for the first 33 years of his life, he also lived and worked there. It came to his attention that rival bar owners were increasingly sending their staff to purchase his father's stylish aperitivo, known as *Bitter all'uso d'Hollanda*, for resale in their premises. He permitted the practice to continue, but only

TO SERVE

Campari has a bittersweet bouquet and taste, which varies depending on the mixers used. Its aromas and sweetness change dramatically, from the crisp dryness of Campari Soda to the medium-dry, even slightly sweet flavor of Campari and orange juice. The five main ways of serving Campari are as follows:

☆ On ice, with a slice of orange

☆ **Campari Soda**, from the classic 1930s premixed bottle

☆ **Camparino**, for which a soda gun with a constant supply of chilled soda is required; it makes a deliciously frothy drink

☆ ⅓ Campari and ⅔ orange juice, with lots of ice. One of the most popular styles, as it is medium-dry

☆ **Campari Shakerato**: Fill a shaker with a good portion of crushed ice and a double measure of Campari. Shake vigorously for 60 seconds, then strain into a glass

☆ **Campari Testarossa**: ½ Campari and ½ Vodka in a tumbler on ice, with an added splash of tonic

Some modernists prefer to drink their Campari tall, with either grapefruit or cranberry juice. Whatever you do, remember to use only slices of orange, as lemon clashes with Campari.

on the understanding that they displayed a sign announcing that they were selling authentic Campari bitters. He therefore, quite innocently, gave birth to the brand's now well-known name.

Quite by chance, a remarkable romance transformed Campari into an international brand. Davide fell head over heels in love with a beautiful opera singer, Lina Cavalieri. He commissioned her portrait and used it in their publicity.

Lina shocked Davide by abruptly informing him that she was going to Nice for a summer booking. Davide desperately sought an excuse to follow her, telling his family that, as the time had come for them to enter the export market, he was going to France for

several months to open their first international depot in Nice. There, he enjoyed his happiest summer, but soon Lina was on the move again, this time to Moscow, where she hastily married Prince Sasa Bariatinskij. A lovesick Gaspare followed, and Russia became Campari's second export market.

Lina Cavalieri

A year and a divorce later, Lina sailed into New York, rising to dizzy heights of fame when cast opposite the great Caruso at the old Metropolitan Opera House. This time, she married a multimillionaire, Robert W. Chanler. The marriage lasted seven days before Lina had a second divorce, and once more the smitten Campari entered a new export market.

Davide died in 1936, but succeeded in building the brand on a major scale. He had taken his father's aperitif from Milan's Galleria to the finest premises on earth, establishing Campari as the world's top-selling bitters, a position it retains today. He achieved this feat by selling style, and at an early stage, the benefits of mixability. He had defied many other bitters producers, who said their drink should only be consumed after meals, and had sold Campari as a tall drink. He was – for his time – a true marketing genius.

The use of poster advertising by Davide Campari can be seen in the first section of this book. His successors continued that practice, but extended their use of publicity to involve other activities. The Campari tram became a great favorite in cities all over Italy and elsewhere in Europe, and was even shipped as far as the United States.

Campari was also one of the first drinks companies to sponsor sporting events, with soccer, cycling, and winter sports being

favored. Currently, Campari advertisements are seen superbly positioned on Grand Prix motor-racing circuits. Recently, and quite appropriately, Campari has also become the main sponsor of the Italian Grand Prix at Monza.

PRODUCTION

The Campari company practices a discreet but rigid regime of secrecy. Its directors regard its bitters' recipe as the ultimate reason for the company's continuing success. Subsequently, it is not possible to identify any of the herbs and spices involved. The full details of the recipe are known only to the company's president. He personally supervises the preparation of the concentrate once a week with the assistance of several trusted employees, each of whom knows just a small number of the key ingredients, with a copy of the recipe securely kept in a bank vault. The production process involves both maceration in spirits and infusion in water, and takes about two months. The resultant concentrate is blended with purified water, neutral alcohol, and a sugar solution, bringing the final drink to 25 percent alcohol by volume. One can only suspect the presence of certain citrus peels

The Campari tram

and wood barks that contribute to its unique, bittersweet taste. Campari has other international production centers, but the blend of ingredients always comes from Italy.

CAMPARI SODA

Over the past 120 years, Milan has developed a reputation for commercial art, a field in which Campari has been most influential. When the artist De Pero created the unique Campari Soda bottle in 1932, the aging Davide Campari saw it as his last opportunity to support creative talent. The result was the world's first premixed drink in a bottle, which soon became a classic with its 3.3 fluid ounce/⅙ pint/100 ml cone-shaped, unlabeled design.

More than 60 years later, the De Pero bottle is still a great favorite. It makes an eye-catching display in the café-bars of the northern Mediterranean, where 75 percent of its sales occurs, and its size and convenience make it both practical and efficient to serve.

CHAMBERY GAUDIN

The French Savoy Vermouth Tradition

When the kingdom of Savoy was divided between France and Italy, in the nineteenth century, its most northerly sector came under French control. At the time, it was already local custom to vinify French vermouth in a dry style, while in the Italian sector of Savoy, a sweet finish was preferred.

PRODUCTION

A small number of minor producers based near Chambery, the capital of French Savoy, found that the nearby Alps yielded many of the herbs required for their recipes. In the foothills and valleys, vineyards produced wines that were quite light and elegant, but didn't have a great deal of flavor. These were used both as base wines for vermouth and to make neutral brandy to fortify the vermouth. Flavoring was provided by alpine flowers and plants, gathered by shepherds and dried in the summer sun. Some of these plants could only be found at high altitudes, and only picked during the brief period when the

 KEY FACTS

COMPOSITION	*A secret recipe of herbs and spices, white wine, and neutral-grape alcohol*
COUNTRY OF ORIGIN	*France*
WHERE PRODUCED	*Chambery, Savoy, France*
PRIME MARKETS	UK, Japan, USA

snow melted. They were then placed in containers to be macerated in the wine, imparting delicate and fragrant flavors. Other wood barks and spices were also used, including the medicinal wormwood bark.

One traditional label which can still be found, albeit less so than before, is vermouth Gaudin, which is a particularly elegant style. The Gaudin brand is still produced in the traditional manner by Routin, a company that specializes in fruit drinks.

TO SERVE

Chambery Gaudin has a pale-gold color and an elegant bouquet, with herbal and floral notes. It is clean and refreshing on the palate, and has a dry finish.

Chambery Gaudin can be served as follows:

☆ Well chilled, with a small slice of lemon peel

☆ Tall, on ice, by mixing with tonic, soda water, or Seven Up/Sprite

☆ As part of a cocktail, such as Vertical on ice: ⅓ vodka or gin, ⅔ vermouth Gaudin, and garnished with a green olive

The Routin plant where Chambery Gaudin vermouth is produced

CINZANO

The Master Distillers

Cinzano gives its foundation date as 1757, the year the Cinzano family were admitted to an official body that they describe as *the University of Master Distillers*. Yet, had they claimed 1568, the year Antonio Cinzano was described in his wedding certificate as a property owner and "producer of elixirs," it would have confirmed them as the oldest of the vermouth-producing houses. Antonio Cinzano was the first in an unbroken family line of drinks producers, which halted

 KEY FACTS

COMPOSITION — *All four Cinzano vermouth styles involve secret recipes of herbs and spices, blended with a lightly fortified wine base*

COUNTRY OF ORIGIN — *Italy*

WHERE PRODUCED — *80 percent of Cinzano is made in Italy. The other 20 percent is produced in Germany and Argentina*

AWARDS — *Gold medals: Florence 1861, London 1862, Paris 1867 & 1889, Philadelphia 1876, Chicago 1883, Melbourne 1880, Buenos Aires 1900. Also, the Papal warrant of Pius X in 1905, and royal warrants for Portugal, Romania, Italy, Spain, Bulgaria, Sweden, and Austria*

VISITORS — *Groups are welcome by prior appointment. Telephone: (39-172) 477170. Visitors to Cinzano at San Vittorio d'Alba can also view their archives, glass collection, and a building that was once owned by the King of Savoy*

abruptly with the accidental death of Alberto Marone Cinzano in 1989.

In 1757, Cinzano moved to their new shop in the Via Dora Grossa in Turin, where they soon developed a reputation for wines, drinks, and, at the end of the eighteenth century, for vermouth. They entered the export markets fairly quickly, and soon were represented in Argentina, Brazil, the United States, all over Europe, India, and various countries in Africa and Asia. In 1863, Cinzano opened cellars amid the vineyards at San Stefano Belbo, and began renting a major property at San Vittorio d'Alba from King Carlo Alberto of Savoy. The latter was purchased in 1893, and remains the company's headquarters. By 1895, there were 250 full-time employees, a figure that grew to 1,500 by the mid 1930s, but which has now decreased to 200. However, due to automation and other modern techniques, these 200 employees are able to produce more volume than the previous 1,500 ever did. From 1902 to after the Second World War, Cinzano had a separate operation at Chambery, France, where it produced a French Dry Vermouth called Mont Blanc.

TO SERVE

Cinzano **Dry** is very pale in color, has some floral notes on the bouquet, and is pleasantly dry, with a delicate, citrus flavor

Cinzano **Rosso** has an intense amber rather than red color, with a sweet, aromatic flavor.

Cinzano **Rosé** is a full, salmon-pink color. It has a vinous bouquet, with camomile being clearly noticeable in the aroma, and is quite sweet on the palate.

Cinzano **Bianco** is a pale-straw color. It is the sweetest and most full-bodied of the range, with a distinctive taste of cloves in the aftertaste. The Cinzano vermouth styles are best served as follows:

Cinzano Dry

☆ On ice, with a slice of lemon

☆ On ice, with soda

Cinzano Rosso

☆ On ice, with a slice of lemon

☆ On ice, with dry ginger ale

Cinzano Rosé

☆ On ice alone

☆ On ice, with tonic (to make it drier)

Cinzano Bianco

☆ On ice, with a slice of lemon

☆ On ice, with bitter lemon

PRODUCTION

Cinzano admit that they have made several changes to their vermouth recipes over the years. In keeping with most other vermouth houses, their first vermouth was red and sweet, and it therefore became necessary to adapt its recipe when its Dry version was introduced in the nineteenth century, and the medium-sweet Bianco in the twentieth. In fact, the new styles didn't require as many herbs and spices. In the 1930s, the Cinzano Rosso recipe was revised to include 35 ingredients, such as marjoram, thyme, musk yarrow, dittany of Crete, and an alpine herb called *Achillea moscata*. The

lighter, more elegant Cinzano Dry requires less flavoring, and only 14 ingredients, with camomile and rose petals being prominent. Cinzano Rosé, which was launched in the 1960s, is much more vinous than the other styles, and one can detect camomile, gentian, and cinnamon in its aroma. Cinzano Bianco contains artemisia, gentian, camomile, and some grapefruit peels, all of which can be detected in its aroma, and it also has some spicy notes of cloves in the aftertaste.

Cinzano implemented a policy at the beginning of the twentieth century of purchasing from an assortment of herb and spice specialists, such as Alphonse Isnard of Paris, Tommaso Carraro of Turin, and the suitably named Carlo Erba of Milan.

At present, all Cinzano ingredients are purchased by its international headquarters in Geneva, Switzerland, where they are first sorted and mixed, and then sent to their production centers in various countries. This practice helps control consistency wherever Cinzano is made.

TO SERVE

Cinzano is also an important component in many well-known cocktails, such as:

GIOTTO
3 parts vodka
3 parts Cinzano Dry
1 part strawberry syrup or cordial
3 parts blended, fresh strawberries

TINTORETTO
1 part Cinzano Rosso
2 parts pale Scotch whisky
Stirred with ice
Served with a cherry

TIZIANO
2 parts Cinzano Bianco
7 parts vodka
1 part bitters
Shaken with lots of ice
Then served in a well-chilled glass
with a few mint leaves

CINZANO BITTER

Cinzano Bitter is similar in character to Campari Bitter, but is a little lighter in style. It is a classic Italian bitters, with an aromatic flavor and a bitter aftertaste. It is 21.5 percent abv, compared with the 25 percent abv of Campari.

PRODUCTION

Cinzano Bitter is produced from a secret recipe of herbs and spices in which gentian, Chinese rhubarb and peppermint are predominant. Both maceration and infusion are involved. The resulting concentrate is then blended with neutral alcohol, sugar, and purified water.

TO SERVE

Cinzano Bitter *has a deep-red color with orange highlights, and possesses a well-balanced aroma of herbs and spices, with distinctive peel flavors. It has a pleasant, bitter aftertaste. It is best served as follows:*

☆ *On ice, with a twist of lemon*

☆ *On ice, with soda or Seven Up/Sprite*

☆ *⅓ Cinzano Bitter with ⅔ orange juice*

 KEY FACTS

COMPOSITION	*Secret recipe of herbs and spices, neutral alcohol, sugar, and purified water*
COUNTRY OF ORIGIN	*Italy*
WHERE PRODUCED	*San Vittorio d'Alba, Italy*
PRIME MARKETS	*Spain*
VISITORS	*Groups by appointment only. Telephone: (39-172) 477170*

CINZANO ORANCIO

It takes many years to establish an aperitivo as more than a passing fashion. Cinzano Orancio, introduced in 1995, seems to have the qualities necessary for survival.

PRODUCTION

Cinzano describe Orancio as an aromatized wine. It comprises 75 percent white wine, sugar, neutral alcohol, and a secret recipe of herbs and spices, in which orange peels are prevalent. Wormwood is not included in its blend.

TO SERVE

Cinzano Orancio is gold-colored with amber hues, and has a delicate bouquet redolent of herbs and orange peels. It is quite smooth on the palate, with a pronounced, sweet-orange flavor.
Cinzano Orancio is best served as follows:

☆ On ice, with a twist of orange peel

☆ On ice, with soda and a twist of orange peel

 KEY FACTS

COMPOSITION	A blend of herbs and spices, with orange peels being predominant
COUNTRY OF ORIGIN	Italy
WHERE PRODUCED	Italy
PRIME MARKETS	Germany, Denmark, Sweden, the Benelux countries, and Italy
VISITORS	As with Cinzano Vermouth, groups by appointment only

COCCHI

Small Brand – Great Tradition

Two of the most original and exclusive of all Italian aperitivos were created by the same man, Giulio Cocchi, in 1891. They are Cocchi Aperitivo Americano and Cocchi Barolo Chinato. The Tuscan-born Cocchi traveled north to Piedmont, settling in the town of Asti (best known for its wines). There, Cocchi built his cellars and began trading. Today the company is owned by the Bava family, who are also highly reputed winemakers in Piedmont.

APERITIVO AMERICANO

Aperitivo Americano is a classic aperitivo with a unique aroma, in which both white wine and orange peels can be detected. It should not be confused with the Americano cocktail, which consists of one part vermouth and one part bitters.

 KEY FACTS

COMPOSITION	A secret blend of herbs and spices (excluding wormwood), and with more bitter- and sweet-orange peels than normal
COUNTRY OF ORIGIN	Italy
WHERE PRODUCED	Cocconato, Piedmont, Italy
WORLDWIDE ANNUAL SALES VOLUME	8,000 bottles
PRIME MARKETS	Italy and California
VISITORS	Welcome (by appointment) at the Bava cellars in Cocconato, where the production is carried out. Telephone: (39-141) 907084

TO SERVE

Aperitivo Americano has a distinctive, vinous aroma, with clear hints of bitter- and sweet-orange peels.
Cocchi Aperitivo Americano can be served as follows:

☆ *On ice, with a slice of orange*

☆ *Tall, with soda and ice*

☆ *With a small measure (10 percent) of Campari Bitters – for a slightly more bitter taste*

☆ *With a small measure (10 percent) of apple juice – for a slightly sweeter taste*

PRODUCTION

The full details of the production of the Aperitivo Americano are only known by its producers, but what can be revealed is that various mountain herbs, flowers, and bitter- and sweet-orange peels are among the ingredients.

BAROLO CHINATO

Barolo Chinato was first marketed by Giulio Cocchi at Asti in 1891, and steadily grew into a major aperitivo within the Italian provinces of Piedmont, Liguria, and Lombardy. Cocchi developed a chain of five production centers, which each had their own bars, known as *Bar Barolo Chinato Cocchi* or just *Bar Cocchi*. One of these can still be seen in Asti. Nowadays, Cocchi first ages the famous red wine of Barolo for five years, then adds the china bark (quinine) with other herbs and spices before aging the blend for at least another five years.

The Cocchi plant, Asti, Piemonte, Italy

PRODUCTION

Apart from Barolo wine, sugar, and alcohol, there are another 24 ingredients, including China bark. The drink is aged in old-oak casks for 12 months – not to add any tannins or flavors, but to allow it to breathe. The result appears to be that the Cocchi label of Barolo Chinato is somewhat more vinous than its competitors.

The secret recipe is known to two of the Bava brothers, Giulio and Paolo, who will only reveal that cardamom, dried orange peels, chinese rhubarb, and gentian are involved.

TO SERVE

Barolo Chinato has a subtle nose of wood barks, with a slightly vinous aroma and a light, bitter aftertaste.
Cocchi Barolo Chinato can be served as follows:

☆ Cellar-cool on its own

☆ On ice, with a slice of orange

 KEY FACTS

COMPOSITION	A secret blend of 24 herbs and spices, with Barolo wine lightly fortified with neutral brandy
COUNTRY OF ORIGIN	Italy
WHERE PRODUCED	Cocconato, Piedmont, Italy
WORLDWIDE ANNUAL SALES VOLUME	10,000 bottles
PRIME MARKETS	Italy and California
VISITORS	Welcome (by appointment) at the Bava cellars in Cocconato, where the production is carried out. Telephone: (39-141) 907084

CYNAR

The Artichoke Medicine

In 1949, a company called Pezziol, based in Padua, northern Italy, launched a spirit-based medicine flavored with artichoke extract. By 1951, sales had reached over one million bottles per annum, and a decision was made to re-launch the successful drink *Cynar*, as an aperitivo. An export drive was launched at the same time, with Switzerland, and later on France, becoming its first international markets.

Subsequently, Cynar moved its headquarters to Termoli in the Abruzzo province of Italy. It is exported to 16 countries, and is the second best-selling bitters in the world after Campari. Cynar is named after *cynarina*, a substance extracted from artichoke leaves, but also contains a number of other herbs and spices.

In its home country, Cynar is generally drunk as a *digestivo*, i.e. after meals. The swing from *aperitivo* to *digestivo* was due to a

 KEY FACTS

COMPOSITION	*Blend of cynarina (artichoke extract) with various herbs and spices, including rhubarb, sweet- and bitter-orange peels, gentian, and a neutral-spirit base*
COUNTRY OF ORIGIN	*Italy*
WHERE PRODUCED	*Termoli, Abruzzo province, Italy*
WORLDWIDE ANNUAL SALES VOLUME	*12 million bottles*
PRIME MARKETS	*Italy, France, Switzerland, Brazil, Japan*

change in consumer perception that took place in the late 1960s and 1970s. In all its other export markets, the majority of its consumers enjoy it as an aperitif before meals. This is a most unusual contrast, bearing in mind the increasing number of Cynar consumers who drink it tall.

In Italy, the Cynar brand name was for years closely associated with a long-running series of television commercials starring a well-known actor, Ernesto Calindri, and relating the health benefits of the artichoke – resulting in a boom for both the vegetable and the aperitif. In 1997, the company started to promote the benefits of mixing Cynar with an assortment of mixers by giving away 155 classic Italian Vespa motorbikes.

TO SERVE

Cynar *has a very distinctive taste, and a bouquet evocative of peels and herbs with a medicinal aroma. Its taste varies on the palate depending on the method of serving, but when consumed on ice without any mixers, it has a slightly sweet, citrus flavor and a light, bitter aftertaste.*

Cynar is a much more versatile drink than many people realize. It is often served in the following ways:

☆ *Straight, poured from a chilled bottle*

☆ *On ice, with a slice of lemon*

☆ *With a generous splash of soda, slice of orange, and ice*

☆ *50/50 Cynar and Cola, with added ice and a slice of lemon or lime*

☆ *50/50 Cynar and tonic water, with added ice and a slice of lemon or lime*

PRODUCTION

As with many well-known aperitifs, the Cynar formula is a secret. What is known is that it is spirit-based, and involves a concoction of herbs and spices, among them the cynarina extract, rhubarb, sweet- and bitter-orange peels, and gentian. This results in an unusual, caramel-brown color.

Artichoke leaves give Cynar its distinctive flavor

DUBONNET

The Parisian Chemist's Recipe

D ubonnet was founded in 1846 by a Parisian chemist, Joseph Dubonnet. He created the drink in response to an appeal from the French government, who were desperate to find a palatable way for troops in North Africa to take quinine as protection against malaria. Legend suggests that the picture of a cat on the Dubonnet label is testimony to the many nights Joseph spent doing his research, leaving his wife to the sole company of her cat.

Joseph Dubonnet succeeded in fortifying white and red wines from the Roussillon region, and blending these with a recipe of herbs and spices, many of which were available in that area. When he commercialized his new wine-based aperitif, he moved his entire operation to Thuir, in the foothills of the

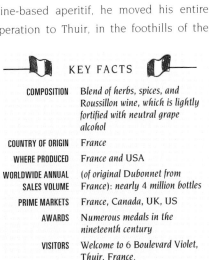

KEY FACTS

COMPOSITION	Blend of herbs, spices, and Roussillon wine, which is lightly fortified with neutral grape alcohol
COUNTRY OF ORIGIN	France
WHERE PRODUCED	France and USA
WORLDWIDE ANNUAL SALES VOLUME	(of original Dubonnet from France): nearly 4 million bottles
PRIME MARKETS	France, Canada, UK, US
AWARDS	Numerous medals in the nineteenth century
VISITORS	Welcome to 6 Boulevard Violet, Thuir, France. Telephone: (33) 468530542

French Pyrenees, where Dubonnet is still produced today in white, amber (gold), and red styles.

Dubonnet Quinquina, as the drink was called for many generations, not only served its medicinal purposes in Morocco, Algeria, and Tunisia, but became a favorite among colonial settlers, and found many followers in the south of France.

In the late 1930s, to attract more visitors to Thuir, the Dubonnet directors embarked on an ambitious scheme to build "the world's largest oak barrel." The project was interrupted by the onset of World War II, and was not completed until 1950. The barrel has a capacity of over 1.3 million bottles, and is one of 800 oak casks in the Dubonnet cellars.

After the war, Dubonnet entered an agreement with the American Schenley Company, giving the US importers authority to adjust the blend to meet American tastes. Eventually, Schenley ac-quired exclusive US rights, which permitted them to produce their own American version of Dubonnet, with different packaging and variations in the recipe.

More recently, the Heaven Hill Company in Kentucky has purchased the US brand, and American Dubonnet is now made in California according to the original French formula. It has also been repackaged to reflect its French heritage. In Canada, the original French style is still imported.

PRODUCTION

As with most other brands, the recipe is a closely guarded secret. Among the key ingredients are quinine from Peru, cinnamon, bitter-orange peels, green coffee beans, and camomile. It is still based on the same Roussillon wines used by Joseph Dubonnet in the last century, with which a *mistelle* has been blended. The latter is made by adding a small volume of neutral grape alcohol to unfermented grape juice. This prevents fermentation and retains the natural grape sugar. It is then fortified with neutral-grape brandy and aged for three years.

TO SERVE

Dubonnet's aroma is reminiscent of herbs and wine, with rich, subtle flavors.
One can recognize vanilla in the bouquet.
It is full on
the palate, with a rich, herbal,
sweet aftertaste.
Dubonnet is best served as follows:

☆ On ice, with a slice of lemon

☆ Tall, on ice with bitter lemon

☆ Tall, on ice with lemonade

NB: Serving four parts of a mixer to 1 part of Dubonnet reduces its alcoholic strength to only 3.7 abv.

KEO

Aperitifs from the Greek Islands

Keo was founded in 1927 in Cyprus, when it took control of the island's first organized winery, which had been established in 1893 by an English family. Later, Keo opened a second winery at Mallia, to be followed soon by its main one at Limassol. Today, the company is the biggest industrial employer on the island with 600 staff.

COMMANDARIA ST. JOHN

In the twelfth century, Cyprus was a favorite place for crusaders to rest on their journeys to and from battles in the Holy Land. Cyprus became a center for the Templars and the Hospitaliers, known as the Knights of the Order of St. John. They found a wine, produced in the foothills of the Troodos mountains, that was not only pleasant to drink, but also had medicinal benefits. They named it *Commanderie* after their headquarters.

PRODUCTION

The name *Cyprus Mana*, which predates the term *Commanderie*, was first recorded in ancient Greece in the eighth century B.C. However, it was another 2,400 years before the first detailed account of its unique wine-making process was written, when Estienne de Lusignan described Commandaria St. John in 1572 A.D. in his book

TO SERVE

Commandaria St. John *is a tawny color, with some amber on the rim. It has a rich, dense nose with hints of caramel, and is full and luscious on the palate, with a sweet, plummy aftertaste. It belongs to the group of fortified wines that can be drunk both as an aperitif and as dessert wine.*

Keo Commandaria St. John should be served cellar-cool.

Metzes are ideal with both Keo Commandaria St. John and Ouzo

Descriptions of the Island of Cyprus: "There is a certain grapevine ... which ripens at the end of July, whose grapes are not gathered until the end of September. They (the grapes) are put on the roofs ... the space of 3 days ... then trodden, and the pips and stalks removed before fermentation." Clearly, he was present at the harvest, but may have left before the aging in large earthenware jars called *mana* that are buried in the soil. Today, Commandaria is still made very much in the same manner, except that for the past two centuries, it has been fortified with grape brandy.

KEY FACTS

COMPOSITION	*Wine and neutral brandy*
COUNTRY OF ORIGIN	*Cyprus*
WHERE PRODUCED	*Kalo Chorio, Troodos mountains, Cyprus*
WORLDWIDE ANNUAL SALES VOLUME	*300,000 bottles per annum*
PRIME MARKETS	*UK, Sweden, and Denmark*
AWARDS	*Numerous gold medals at various exhibitions, including Budapest 1958, Brussels 1963, Yalta 1970, Leipzig 1971, Club Oenologique, England, 1974 and 1978*
VISITORS	*Tours daily at 10.00 a.m. Telephone: (357-5) 362053*

KEO OUZO

Keo Ouzo is a versatile drink but its main role is as an aperitif to be enjoyed with an array of *metzes* (small appetizers).

PRODUCTION

Ouzo is far less complex than pastis and has a grape-alcohol base, whereas pastis uses neutral alcohol. Ouzo is produced by macerating some of the aromatic plants in grape alcohol and distilling others, including aniseed, in pot stills. The aniseed is made into an oil concentrate and blended with other plant extracts and a sugar solution.

TO SERVE

When diluted with chilled water, **Keo Ouzo** becomes milky, evoking an aroma of aniseed. On the palate, it is reminiscent of herbs, and leaves a refreshing aftertaste.

Keo Ouzo is usually consumed as follows:

☆ One part ouzo to five parts chilled water

☆ On ice, with black-currant and other similar fruit juices, or with lemonade

 KEY FACTS

COMPOSITION	Anise and other herbs, neutral grape alcohol, sugar solution, and purified water
COUNTRY OF ORIGIN	Cyprus
WHERE PRODUCED	Limassol, Cyprus
PRIME MARKETS	UK, USA, and Germany
VISITORS	Daily tours at Keo in Limassol are available; telephone: (357-5) 362053

LILLET

The Bordeaux Aperitif

illet, also called Lillé, was first produced in 1887 in the village of Podensac, in the Graves wine region of Bordeaux. It was created by two brothers, Paul and Raymond Lillet, who had been running a wine business there for 15 years. Skilfully blending white and red wines with fruit extracts, they developed both a white and a red style. Lillet enjoyed considerable success, but as with many other aperitifs, its popularity faded in the last two decades. Now, more than a century after its birth, it is enjoying a revival.

White Lillet, described by its producers as a "French Aperitif wine," is more widely available than the red, though the latter is more popular in America. Lillet, the only major Bordeaux wine-based aperitif, was first shipped to the United States at the turn of the century. It enjoyed a revival when Prohibition ended. A

 KEY FACTS

COMPOSITION	*A secret recipe of fruits and spices, Bordeaux A.C. wine, and brandy*
COUNTRY OF ORIGIN	*France*
WHERE PRODUCED	*Podensac, near Bordeaux, France*
PRIME MARKETS	*USA and France*
AWARDS	*Gold medal International Wine and Spirit Competition, London 1995*
VISITORS	*Visitors are welcome from Monday through Friday all-year-round, and seven days a week from June 15 through September 15. Telephone: (33) 556274142*

TO SERVE

Lillet Blanc has a deep-gold color and a bouquet with initial floral notes, followed by a citrus aroma and minor traces of mint. It is fresh, quite vinous and full-bodied in the mouth, and has a fairly long, distinctive finish with an aftertaste of peels. Lillet Rouge has a deep, red-wine color, with a powerful bouquet of ripe fruit and hints of spices. It is full and rich on the palate. All Lillet styles are best served as follows:

☆ Chilled, in a white-wine glass, with the option of a twist of lemon or orange peel

☆ On ice, with tonic, soda, or sparkling water, and garnished with a slice of orange

☆ Lillet Special: Two drops of Angostura Bitters on an ice cube in a wine glass, topped with Lillet Blanc. Garnish with a slice of fruit and a sprig of mint.

special deluxe version of the aperitif, known as La Reserve Jean de Lillet, is also available, and is claimed to be the only single vintage aperitif still produced. Blended from selected wines and fruit liqueurs, La Reserve Jean de Lillet is aged in oak barrels, and – most unusual for an aperitif – left to mature for a few years after bottling.

PRODUCTION

Lillet Blanc is produced from Semillon and Sauvignon Blanc grapes from the Bordeaux appellation contrôlée region. It is made to a secret recipe that involves macerating fruits in brandy for four to six months. Subsequently, ten different fruit concentrates are blended with the wines, and the resulting drink is then left to settle and mature for a period of six to eight months. The wine content is 85 percent, and the fruit concentrate provides 15 percent of the volume. No herbs or spices are used.

Lillet Rouge follows the same principles, except that Cabernet Sauvignon and Merlot grape varieties from the Bordeaux vineyards are used.

La Reserve Jean de Lillet is made in a similar manner, but is aged both in small oak barrels and in bottles.

MARIE BRIZARD
GUIGNOLET

A Rare French Classic

Guignolet has an unusual history, for it developed simultaneously in several regions of France as an *aperitif paysan* (country aperitif) made from unripe cherries. Later, it was commercialized by a few companies as a liqueur, before post-war consumers decided it was best drunk on ice as an aperitif. Today, it is fairly difficult to find, and the best-known example comes from the celebrated house of Marie Brizard.

PRODUCTION

The commercial producers of Guignolet didn't take long to realize that they would obtain superior results by using sour and bittersweet varieties of naturally ripened cherries. For example, Marie Brizard Guignolet is made with small, sour cherries grown in the mountains near Lyons, and

KEY FACTS

COMPOSITION	*Cherries, sugar solution, and neutral alcohol*
COUNTRY OF ORIGIN	*France*
WHERE PRODUCED	*Bordeaux, France*
PRIME MARKETS	*France and some Northern European countries*
VISITORS	*Visitors are welcome to Marie Brizard's, where various drinks, including Guignolet, are produced. Telephone: (33) 556018585*

other bittersweet cherries, known as "Burlat Bigarreau," which come from the renowned Burgundy region.

First, the whole cherries are macerated in neutral alcohol for 15 days. This produces what is known as "the drained juice." Then, the cherries are removed from the alcohol and crushed, providing "the pressed juice." The next stage involves blending both juices and leaving them to marry for a few days. Afterwards, the combined juice is filtered, slightly sweetened, and bottled immediately in order to retain freshness. The resulting Guignolet is a completely natural drink, without any coloring agents or additives.

TO SERVE

Marie Brizard Guignolet has a bright, cherry-red color and a fresh, fruity bouquet. On the palate, it has a delicious, bittersweet flavor and quite a long, slightly sweet finish.
Marie Brizard Guignolet should be served on ice.

Cherry tree in blossom

MARTINI

The Giant

Martini & Rossi is the giant among vermouth producers, and has been a substantial operator since its foundation, which the company gives as 1863. However, its origins can be traced back to 1847, when four prosperous men called Michel, Re, Agnelli, and Baudino formed a business called The National Distillery for Wine and Spirits in what was then the Kingdom of Piedmont and Sardinia. By the early 1850s, the company was thriving, with offices in Sardinia and in France. A major influence in this success was its young commercial director, Alessandro Martini, who possessed both a keen

 KEY FACTS

COMPOSITION	A blend of numerous alpine herbs and tropical spices, with a wine-base fortified with neutral alcohol
COUNTRY OF ORIGIN	Italy
WHERE PRODUCED	All herbs and spices are blended in Geneva, Switzerland, and then distributed to Martini production centers in Italy, Spain, France, Switzerland, Brazil, Uruguay, Argentina, and Chile, and two independent centers that produce it under license in Hungary and South Africa
PRIME MARKETS	Italy, USA, UK, Russia, Spain, France, and Germany
AWARDS	Numerous medals from various countries displayed on label and building
VISITORS	The Martini plant at Pessione and the Martini Wine Museum can be visited by appointment only. Telephone: (39-11) 94191

business brain and a professional know-ledge of wine and drink production, especially of vermouth and bitters. By coincidence, in the 1830s, he had been an apprentice *maître licoriste* training alongside another aperitivo pioneer, Gaspare Campari, at the Bass bar in Turin.

Alessandro Martini

By 1863, the company had been restructured. Re died, and the other three original directors had withdrawn – Agnelli's descendants were later to become famous in their own right for the Fiat Car company and the Juventus soccer club. Alessandro Martini and newcomer Teofilo Sola had joined the board, and had invited a wine expert named Luigi Rossi to help them develop a major vermouth brand. Since Martini and Rossi started working together in 1863, the company chose that year as its foundation date. It seems almost certain that the business produced a vermouth before this date, but no reliable evidence has survived. What is generally ack-nowledged is that Luigi Rossi was responsible for creating the recipe for the Martini Rosso (Red) vermouth, which is still sold today.

At the time, competition was fierce in the Italian vermouth market, so the directors decided to build their label as a major export brand. As a result of this decision, the business was moved to a massive new plant, which they constructed at Pessione, south of Turin. They carefully selected a site right alongside the new Turin-Genoa railway line, and obtained authority to take their own railway siding from the main line and run it adjacent to the warehouses, where they could load cases of vermouth directly into wagons. Soon, the quaysides at Genoa were busy with vermouth en route to new markets.

In 1871, Teofilo Sola resigned from the company, which was then re-named Martini & Rossi. By this time, Alessandro Martini had implemented the policy of entering their vermouth in competitions held throughout Europe. In 1865, it won a gold medal at Dublin, in 1873, one at Vienna, and another at the Exposition Universelle in Paris in 1878. This led to favorable publicity in those major markets, and added to the brand's prestige on the world stage, for as quickly as the medals were won, Martini ordered the reprinting of the vermouth's label, with replicas of each new medal proudly displayed.

In 1997, the Martini vermouth label underwent a major revision for the first time in over a century. Its upper half still displays a great deal of the company's heritage, but the lower section has acquired a more contemporary design. At the top of the label is Vittoria, the mythological Roman goddess of victory, blowing her trumpet over the flags of many countries where Martini has conquered the national markets. Just below Vittoria is the bull of Turin, the city's traditional coat of arms, and also the Italian royal coat of arms.

MARTINI EXTRA-DRY VERMOUTH

Many writers have suggested that Martini Extra-Dry didn't evolve until well into the twentieth century, but new evidence now shows that it was first developed in 1890, especially for the Cuban market. The company was trying to make progress there, but encountered some serious opposition from the French Dry Vermouth company, Noilly Prat, which it now owns. Martini's Cuban agent suggested that the company should blend an extra-dry white vermouth to compete in his market. His advice was followed, and the response was extremely favorable. The Extra-Dry was then selected for various test markets, such as Turkey and Egypt. However, it was withdrawn after about ten years, only to return later on a more widespread, international scale.

The old Martini factory

PRODUCTION

The quality of the vermouth produced at the end of the twentieth century is undoubtedly better than it was in the middle of the nineteenth century. This is because the cultivation of the ingredients and the production of wine and neutral spirits has improved considerably in the meantime.

At its modernized Pessione cellars, Martini produces its vermouths in two main stages. During the first, the required flavorings are extracted from the herbs and spices, and then blended into a concentrate. Ingredients include mugwort, lemon leaves, sage, sandalwood, pine thistle, and marjoram. They are fragmented before being macerated in alcohol for 15–20 days. During the second stage, the wines that Martini & Rossi purchase from Emilia Romagna, Puglia, and Sicily are clarified and filtered. The result is a slightly sparkling wine, to which the aromatic concentrate is added. It is then lightly fortified with neutral alcohol, and sugar and purified water are added to the blend.

The number of herbs and spices varies, depending on the different styles, with more aromatic flavoring for Rosso (or red vermouth) and less for Extra-Dry.

TO SERVE

Martini Extra-Dry *has a very pale, gold color, and an elegant bouquet with some floral notes. It is tangy and dry on the palate, and its aftertaste is reminiscent of peels.*

Martini Rosso *has a deep-amber color and a pungent bouquet. It is complex in the mouth, with a long finish in which herbs and a hint of sweetness can be detected.*

Martini Bianco *has a pale-gold color, with hints of flowers and citrus peels in the bouquet. It is smooth and fairly sweet on the palate.*

Martini Rosé *is a salmon-pink color, and has a rich, vinous nose with some herbal undertones. It is fairly full on the palate, with a long, clean finish.*

The different types of Martini are best served as follows:

Martini Extra-Dry
☆ *On ice, with a slice of lemon*

☆ *On ice, with tonic, soda, or Seven Up/Sprite to taste*

Martini Rosso
☆ *On ice, with a slice of lemon or orange*

☆ *On ice, with ginger ale*

Martini Bianco
☆ *On ice, with a slice of lemon*

☆ *On ice, with tonic, soda, or Seven Up/Sprite to taste*

Martini Rosé
☆ *On ice*

The different Martini styles

NOILLY PRAT

Vermouth with a Dash of Romance

In 1800, Joseph Noilly, with the help of his son Louis, began trading in the small port of Marseillan, about 100 miles east of Marseilles. Using local white wines, plus a combination of herbs, spices, and young brandy, he started making the first-ever French dry vermouth to compete with the sweet, Turin styles of vermouth that had been emerging over a generation. In 1811, Louis succeeded his father, and was soon joined in partnership by a mysterious Englishman, Claudius Prat, in 1813 – the date that appears on the Noilly Prat label.

The partnership and the unique name of the drink are the result of a romance. Louis Noilly had a beautiful, dark-eyed daughter who was the object of much attention from local young men, whom Louis suspected were rather more interested in his money than in

KEY FACTS

COMPOSITION	A secret recipe of 12 herbs, white wines, and neutral-grape brandy
COUNTRY OF ORIGIN	France
WHERE PRODUCED	Marseillan, France
WORLDWIDE ANNUAL SALES VOLUME	4,200,000 bottles
PRIME MARKETS	France, USA, Scandinavia
AWARDS	Silver Medal, International Wine & Spirit Competition, 1996, London
VISITORS	Telephone: (33) 46777 2015

her. So he let it be known that any man desiring her hand in marriage must first come and work in his wine business. As Louis threatened to be a hard taskmaster, the young suitors of Marseillan faded from sight. Then one day, a young English traveler named Claudius Prat arrived in the little town, met Louis' lovely daughter, and fell instantly in love. He accepted the terms set down by Louis, and two years later, when the couple married, father-in-law and son-in-law formed a partnership.

PRODUCTION

Noilly Prat French Dry Vermouth was marketed as a completely original style by changing three of the basic stages of vermouth production. The first change affected the extract recipe, the second, the type of wine used, and the third involved an additional aging process, known locally as *vin cuit* (cooked wine). To contrast the Noilly style with the existing Turin vermouths, the secret recipe of herbs and spices was modified to include flowers and fruits available locally. The second change involved using dry wines made from the Picpoul and Clairette varieties from the Languedoc region. A *mistelle* – pure-grape juice fortified with neutral brandy – was added to the blend to act as a natural

Noilly Prat is aged outdoors for 12 months in oak barrels

sweetener. Lastly, after macerating and blending the ingredients, the vermouth was taken in small oak barrels to a large courtyard and left outdoors for 12 months to experience all the climatic extremes of temperature, humidity, and barometric pressure. The local winemakers coined the term *vin cuit*, because on warm days, the contents of the barrels became very hot indeed. One year's exposure to the elements is reputed to equal four years' aging. Finally, when the barrels were brought back into the cellars, their contents were poured into giant blending vats and fortified. Afterwards, the blend was left to mature for a further 12 months before filtration and bottling. From beginning to end, the whole production process takes three years.

Visitors to Noilly Prat at Marseillan today can see these very same processes just as they were 200 years ago. The only real change is that the local wines are of a much higher quality today than they were originally.

Noilly Prat Red Vermouth is also marketed on a much lesser scale than the white version, and therefore in some countries is not even available.

TO SERVE

Noilly Prat has a pale, golden color. It is more vinous on the nose than most Italian vermouths, and includes some floral notes. It has a crisp, dry, distinctive palate, and its tangy aftertaste offers hints of citrus peels.

Noilly Prat is best served as follows:

☆ With ice, and a slice of lemon in a wide-rimmed glass

☆ With ice, and a choice of mixers in a tall glass

☆ With tonic water, for a simple yet delicious drink

☆ With ice, and gin or vodka

PASTIS 51

The Marseilles Tradition

Pastis 51 – so called because it was launched in 1951 – is a classic example of the traditional, heavily licorice-flavored pastis from the Marseilles area in the south of France. It is owned by the Pernod-Ricard company, who market it as an alternative to their two flagship brands, Pernod and Ricard.

PRODUCTION

As with similar pastis, the recipe of Pastis 51 is confidential but it clearly involves star anise, licorice and other herbs and spices. One acknowledged ingredient is cola beans, which may be the flavoring that distinguishes Pastis 51 from its counterparts. Its production process involves macerating powdered licorice twigs in a mixture of aniseed extract, water, alcohol and sugar; a sweet note comes from licorice which is the most important factor

 KEY FACTS

COMPOSITION	*Aniseed, licorice, other herbs and spices, caramel, neutral alcohol, sugar syrup, and water*
COUNTRY OF ORIGIN	*France*
WHERE PRODUCED	*Marseilles and Creteil near Paris, France*
WORLDWIDE ANNUAL SALES VOLUME	*Six million bottles*
PRIME MARKETS	*France, Spain, and Italy*
VISITORS	*Visitors are welcome at 120 Avenue Marechal Foch, 94015 Creteil, France. Telephone: (33) 149815802*

in its preparation. After blending, Pastis 51 is filtered and then bottled.

A peculiarity of Pastis 51 is that it is marketed throughout the world at 45 percent abv (alcohol by volume), except in Belgium, where it is 40 percent abv. Of course, the initial alcohol level of a pastis is not a

> ## TO SERVE
>
> **P**astis 51 has a light-yellow, opaque color when diluted with water. It has an aromatic nose, with anise and other herbs being predominant. Licorice is recognizable on the slightly sweet palate. Pastis 51 is best served as follows:
>
> ☆ One part Pastis 51 to five parts chilled water
>
> ☆ Tall, on ice, with a mixer of choice
>
> ☆ Chilled, with blackcurrant juice, cordial, or creme de cassis

Licorice

direct guide to the actual amount of alcohol consumed, as it is not meant to be drunk straight, and when diluted with water on a ratio of 1/5, as it usually is, its level falls to nine percent abv.

PASTIS JANOT

Pastis in the Marseilles Tradition

P astis Janot is quite a rarity in the world of pastis. It comes from a small producer, who began making a Marseilles-style pastis, i.e., lightly colored and powerfully flavored with licorice roots, in 1928, a few years before Paul Ricard began to attract fame to the region's pastis. Janot is still made in the family-operated distillery at Aubagne, just to the east of Marseilles.

PRODUCTION

The first stage involves macerating herbs and spices – among them, star anise, licorice, cilantro, and nutmeg – for three weeks in a blend of neutral alcohol, purified water, and sugar cane. During this period, the pastis acquires its fine aromas and mouth-watering flavors. The finished drink has a high alcohol level of 45 percent abv.

 KEY FACTS

COMPOSITION	*Various herbs and spices, alcohol, purified water, and cane sugar*
COUNTRY OF ORIGIN	*France*
WHERE PRODUCED	*Aubagne, near Marseilles*
PRIME MARKET	*France*
VISITORS	*Visitors are welcome at Distillerie Janot, Avenue du Pastres, Zone Industrielle les Paluds, BP 1103, 13782 Aubagne.*
	Telephone: (33) 442822957

TO SERVE

Pastis Janot takes on a pale-yellow, cloudy color when diluted with chilled water. It has a bouquet that is redolent of anise and licorice, which are also prominent on the palate. It leaves a refreshing aftertaste, in which herbs are detectable.

Pastis Janot is best drunk in the same way as most classic pastis, i.e. one part Janot to five parts chilled water.

Pastis Janot can also be drunk as follows:

☆ Tall

☆ On ice

☆ With Seven Up/Sprite

☆ With black currant cordial

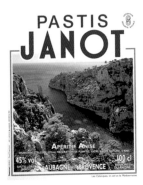

PERNOD

Doctor Ordinaire's Absinthe

When the French Revolution broke out with its reign of terror, thousands of French loyalists hastily sought exile in nearby countries. One elderly emigré to the Valais region of Switzerland was Dr. Ordinaire, a retired scientist who escaped with many of his possessions and his trusted housekeeper. He settled in the town of Couvet around 1790. To prevent the decline of his mental faculties, he set out to create an original drink, using only ingredients from his new location.

After a lengthy period of experimentation, he invited friends and neighbors to try the final product, which he termed *absinthe*. Its name was derived from one of the main ingredients, the so-called wormwood bark, from its Latin name, *Artemisia absinthium*. Also prominent in its recipe was the star-anise plant.

 KEY FACTS

COMPOSITION	*Spirit-based, with star anise, fennel, a little licorice extract, and other herbs*
COUNTRY OF ORIGIN	*Switzerland. Production later moved to France*
WHERE PRODUCED	*La Pernoderie, 120 Avenue du Maréchal Foch, 94015 Créteil, Paris, France*
ALCOHOL BY VOLUME	*40 percent*
WORLDWIDE ANNUAL SALES VOLUME	*7.7 million bottles*
PRIME MARKETS	*France, Germany, UK*
VISITORS	*Welcome; for enquiries, telephone: (33) 49815802*

On his death, Dr. Ordinaire bequeathed both the recipe for his absinthe and a substantial sum of money to his housekeeper, with the advice that she should invest it in a property where she could both produce the drink and establish a bar to sell it. She carried out his suggestions, and quietly began to advertise the drink as Dr. Ordinaire's Absinthe. One auspicious day, two other French

French Revolution crowd surges toward the Hotel de Ville

emigrés, Major Henri Dubois and his son-in-law, Henri-Louis Pernod, visited the bar for a drink, and were so delighted that they later returned and made her an offer for the business. The former housekeeper accepted, and later retired comfortably.

In the meantime, the political situation in France had stabilized, and royalist exiles were permitted to return. Among them were Major Dubois and Henri-Louis Pernod. They resettled in the small town of Doubs, near Pontarlier in the mountainous Jura region, where the star anise plant could be easily found, and together they commenced production of their absinthe there.

Soon, sales of Dr. Ordinaire's Absinthe spread across France. By the latter part of the nineteenth century, as the great cabarets, such as the Moulin Rouge and the Folies Bergères, in Paris, attracted a newly prosperous generation, the distinctive absinthe, which became cloudy when mixed with water, established itself as the fashionable drink in the French capital. But early in the twentieth century, it was reported that heavy consumers of absinthe had suffered permanent mental damage, and the drink was banned in the United States and other countries. A deadly chemical, known as *Tujone*, was identified in the wormwood bark, which was responsible for the mental deterioration.

The Pernod family went back to basics, producing a new recipe for a drink that had a similar appearance to absinthe when diluted.

Its recipe included star anise, fennel, various aromatic herbs, and a small quantity of a light licorice extract. A new label was printed identifying it as Pernod Anise, and its marketing began.

Suddenly the Pernod family received news that another small aperitif producer in the south of France – also called Pernod, but unrelated to them – was taking legal action to prevent them using the name. A court hearing was imminent until the Pernod's family lawyer, a Monsieur Hemard, made a remarkable proposal. He suggested the two parties form a partnership. Hemard himself would become a shareholder. The deal was made, and the new Pernod company began trading. Within a couple of years, the aperitif from southern France was withdrawn, and all efforts were

> ## TO SERVE
>
> Pernod has an aromatic bouquet, with aniseed being the most distinctive element. It is extremely fresh on the palate, and has a dry finish. The addition of mixers varies the taste accordingly. Consumers of Pernod are divided into two camps: those who prefer the traditional French way of drinking it with chilled water, and the modernists, who enjoy it served tall with mixers.
> Serve Pernod as follows:
>
> ☆ Traditional: 1 part Pernod to 5 parts chilled water (but no ice)
>
> ☆ With ice, and topped with water to taste
>
> ☆ Tall with white lemonade and ice
>
> ☆ With black currant juice and ice

concentrated on producing Pernod Anise. Today, Daniel Hemard, the grandson of the visionary lawyer, is the Président-Directeur-Général of the Pernod company within the Pernod-Ricard group.

PRODUCTION

Two herbs give Pernod its distinctive flavor, star anise and fennel. The herbs undergo a process known as rectification, whereby they are soaked in neutral alcohol and distilled twice, to obtain an oil called anethol. This oil is then combined with extract of licorice and other herbs and plants. Finally, all the ingredients are blended with a mixture of purified water, sugar, and neutral alcohol.

PICON

L'Amer Africain

Gaetan Picon was born in 1809, and after serving his apprenticeship in distilleries in Aix, Toulon, and Marseilles, joined the French army to fight in Algeria. It was here, under the blazing African sun, that he created his bitters in response to the demand from the troops for a thirst-quenching drink. It was a low-alcohol drink flavored with orange peel, quinquina, and bitter-plant extracts; it proved so popular that in 1837, he set up his first distillery in a humble Algerian village, which later became the town of Philippeville. At that time, he called his drink Amer Africain. Further distilleries sprang up in Constantine, Annaba (Bone), and Algiers.

When the French army returned to France in 1870, they took their bitters with them, and Gaetan followed suit. In 1872, he established a factory at the Boulevard National in Marseilles, and began pro-

 KEY FACTS

COMPOSITION	Alcohol, orange peel, quinquina, gentian
COUNTRY OF ORIGIN	France
WHERE PRODUCED	Marseilles, France
WORLDWIDE ANNUAL SALES VOLUME	3,500,000 1-liter bottles
PRIME MARKETS	France, Italy
AWARDS	A diploma won in the Strasbourg Colonial Exhibition
VISITORS	Visitors are welcome. For details, telephone: (33) 241315000

ducing his renamed *Amer Picon*. In 1995, after extensive market research, Picon was relaunched as two brands, Picon Bière and Picon Club, the former to be mixed with light beers and lagers, the latter with dry white wine. Nowadays, Picon claims 80 percent of the French market in brown bitters.

PRODUCTION

Fresh orange peel is macerated in neutral alcohol, mixed with dried orange peel, and then distilled. The dried roots of gentian are macerated separately, and so is

A Picon poster celebrating the company's 100th anniversary

the quinquina. These make up the drink's three key ingredients. Other components include sugar syrup and caramel.

TO SERVE

Picon Bière, *straight, has an almost caramel-brown hue, and a distinctly vegetal nose, in which orange peel is predominant. It has a bittersweet, slightly medicinal aftertaste. It was developed as a result of the practice, popular in northern France, of mixing Amer Picon with beer. It can be served as follows:*

☆ *As le Picon Bière:*
¼ cup/6 tsp/2½ fluid ounces/3 cl Picon and ⅞ cup/7½ fluid ounces/220 ml/22cl beer

Picon Club *is more popular in the wine-growing regions of southern France, where it is mixed with white wine. Serve it as follows:*

☆ *One part Picon to five parts white wine*

Picon can also be served in the original style:

☆ *Chilled on ice, with tonic*

☆ *Chilled on ice, with soda*

☆ *Chilled on ice, with a slice or orange or lemon*

PIMM'S No.1 CUP

Pimm's Oyster Bar

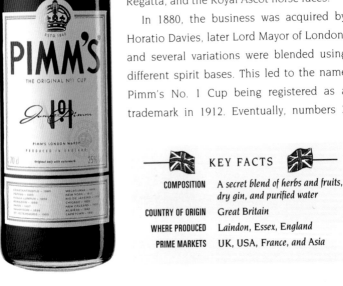

Nobody knows for sure when this classic English drink was created, but in 1823, a certain James Pimm acquired the Hogshead Tavern near the Bank of England in the City of London and converted it to Pimm's Oyster Bar. There he developed a house cup (drink) made from his own recipe of herbs, bitter and sweet spices, and a gin base. Originally, it was only sold in glasses and jugs across the bar, but in 1859, Pimm began selling it in pint bottles at three shillings each. In 1865, he sold the business and the right to use his name to Frederick Sawyer, who proceeded to commercialize and then export the drink. It became a great favorite at prominent social sporting events in England, such as the Wimbledon Tennis Championships, the Henley Rowing Regatta, and the Royal Ascot horse races.

In 1880, the business was acquired by Horatio Davies, later Lord Mayor of London, and several variations were blended using different spirit bases. This led to the name Pimm's No. 1 Cup being registered as a trademark in 1912. Eventually, numbers 2

KEY FACTS

COMPOSITION	*A secret blend of herbs and fruits, dry gin, and purified water*
COUNTRY OF ORIGIN	*Great Britain*
WHERE PRODUCED	*Laindon, Essex, England*
PRIME MARKETS	*UK, USA, France, and Asia*

TO SERVE

Pimm's No. 1 Cup *is one of those very few drinks that — like Angostura Bitters — is never drunk on its own. It has a bouquet that evokes herbs and peels, and is bittersweet on the palate. Because of the many ways of mixing it, the final taste depends on the other drinks, mixers, and ingredients added. It does not really belong to a specific category among aperitifs, but one could say it was related to bitters.*
The following are popular ways to serve Pimm's:

☆ **Classic Pimm's**: *Pour a generous measure of Pimm's No. 1 in a tall glass with ice and Seven Up/Sprite, and garnish the drink with a slice of lemon and a sprig of mint*

☆ **Pimm's Fruit Cup**: *As for Classic Pimm's, but also add slices of apple, orange (or any type of fruit you like), and cucumber. Don't forget the mint*

☆ **Pimm's American**: *Pour one generous measure of Pimm's No. 1, top up with 3 measures of ginger ale, then add a slice of lemon and a sprig of mint*

to 6 were developed using whiskey, brandy, rum, rye whiskey, and vodka. Today, only Pimm's No. I is widely drunk, but Pimm's Vodka Base, previously called No. 6, is available in increasing distribution.

PRODUCTION

The gin base is an old nineteenth-century Booth's London Gin recipe, which has a dry finish. Extracts of various herbs and fruits, purified water, and a secret liqueur are added to the base.

PUNT E MES

The Original Vermouth Producer

Punt e Mes, from Carpano, is regarded by many aficionados as *the* classic vermouth. The house of Carpano was founded in 1786 in Piedmont, Italy, by Antonio Benedetto Carpano, who is widely acknowledged as the creator of the first vermouth recipe. He achieved this by blending various herbs and spices, including wormwood, with wine and brandy.

Punt e Mes may well be the only example of a stockbroker having accidentally created and named an aperitivo. It happened one evening in 1870 in the Carpano bar in Turin, and illustrates the old practice of mixing another bitter or sweet drink with vermouth to suit one's own taste. When the man, deep in conversation about the fluctuations of the Turin stock exchange, ordered his drink, instead of saying "one measure of vermouth with half of bitters," in stock-market jargon, he showed one and a half fingers and said "punt e mes," which is the Piedmontese dialect for "one and a half points."

 KEY FACTS

COMPOSITION	*A secret recipe of over 50 herbs and spices, in which various fruit peels are particularly influential*
COUNTRY OF ORIGIN	*Italy*
WHERE PRODUCED	*Italy*

PRODUCTION

Punt e Mes is a vermouth with a distinctive, bittersweet-orange aftertaste. Its recipe – of over 50 herbs and spices – is said to be shared equally among three people, their knowledge being mutually exclusive. While that secrecy is preserved, it is clear that wormwood and a mixture of bitter- and sweet-orange peels are included, and that various flowers, roots, wood barks, and nuts are also most likely present.

TO SERVE

Punt e Mes has a deep-garnet color and a bouquet of bittersweet peels, confirmed by the full flavor of the palate. Its delicious aftertaste tastes a bit like marmalade. Serve as follows:

☆ Straight and well chilled

☆ On ice, with a slice of orange

☆ On ice, with a slice of orange and soda water

☆ On ice, with tonic water

☆ On ice, with ginger ale

RICARD

A Remarkable Drink from a Remarkable Man

In 1932, in Marseilles, France, 23-year-old Paul Ricard founded the Ricard company to launch a new, aniseed-flavored drink. It was a spirit-based aperitif produced in the local tradition, with its blend matching licorice with star anise, fennel, and various herbs from Provence, and finally sweetened with caramel.

In the course of his career, Ricard saw the company, which he built into the Pernod-Ricard group, become one of the largest drinks producers in the world, owning brands ranging from Jacob's Creek from Australia, to Etchart in Argentina, Irish Distillers in the Republic of Ireland, Ricard and Suze from France, and Ramazzotti from Italy.

Ricard had an uncanny ability to attract attention to his brand. In 1948, he had the

  KEY FACTS

COMPOSITION	*Star anise, fennel, licorice, and other herbs with a spirit base*
COUNTRY OF ORIGIN	*France*
WHERE PRODUCED	*The two bases are made at Bessan in France and blended in various countries*
ALCOHOL BY VOLUME	*45 percent*
WORLDWIDE ANNUAL SALES VOLUME	*84 million bottles*
PRIME MARKET	*France*
VISITORS	*As the drink is produced in stages in different places, visits to see the production process are not possible*

TO SERVE

Ricard has a richer color than most of its competitors, and a bouquet in which licorice and aniseed are evident. It is full of flavor on the palate, with licorice again being prominent.

The distinctive, triangular shape of the Ricard water bottle is part of the Ricard serving ritual. In tens of thousands of French bars, the bottles are carefully stacked in large refrigerators to take up a minimum of space. This allows waiters to produce perfectly chilled water in an instant, and then place a classic design piece on the customers' table. Ricard recommend serving their pastis as follows:

☆ 1 part Ricard to 5 parts water

brilliant idea of putting a Ricard show on the road, following the Tour de France bicycle race from city to city for a month. By the time the cyclists, their teams, their fans, and the masses of journalists arrived, the name Ricard was everywhere. In 1956, during the controversial Suez crisis, supplies of alcoholic drinks were unable to reach the French troops in Egypt, due to a gas shortage. Paul Ricard used his initiative to correct this situation, hiring several camel trains to deliver the craved pastis to the thirsty legionnaires. In 1966, he inaugurated the Ricard Foundation for Oceanography, and in 1970, opened the Paul Ricard Car Racing Track, which today hosts the French Grand Prix. In 1984, the one-billionth bottle of Ricard was sold; two years later, the brand became the third largest-selling drinks brand in the world.

PRODUCTION

The production of Ricard has four stages. The first two stages take place at its Bessan plant in the south of France. These involve extracting the natural oils from fennel and the star-anise plant to make the base ingredient, and then crushing licorice roots that are put onto a screen within a sealed vat, where a powerful water-and-alcohol flow extracts their natural juices. It is this licorice extract that provides Ricard with its instantly recognizable amber color. These bases are then shipped from Bessan to the company's production centers elsewhere in France and abroad, where the third stage takes place. The two basic ingredients are mixed together with various aromatic herbs, double-distilled neutral alcohol, purified water, a sugar solution, and caramel. This stage involves macerating the herbs in alcohol and then blending them. Finally, the drink is filtered three times to enhance its purity. The exact recipe of herbs and spices remains the purely confidential knowledge of the company's directors.

RICCADONNA

From Piedmont to Russia

Ottavio Riccadonna founded his company to produce vermouth and sparkling wine in 1921 in Canelli, in the heart of the Asti vineyards. By the 1930s, other members of his family had joined him, and the house of Riccadonna was thriving to the extent that it began production in South America.

By the mid-sixties, Riccadonna was the third best-selling vermouth, with its own television advertising campaign, a production of around 24 million bottles per annum, and an export market of 35 countries.

In the early 1960s, President Kruschev implemented a policy to reduce drunkenness in Russia. He was particularly anxious about the heavy consumption of vodka and sought

 KEY FACTS

COMPOSITION	*40 herbs and spices, wine, and neutral alcohol*
COUNTRY OF ORIGIN	*Italy*
WHERE PRODUCED	*Canelli, Italy*
ALCOHOL BY VOLUME	*Varies for different countries*
PRIME MARKETS	*Italy, Denmark, Switzerland, and some Eastern European countries*
AWARDS	*Numerous gold medals from Turin, Klostenberg, Sofia, and Lublijana, and the 1943 Papal warrant of Pope Pius XII*
VISITORS	*Visitors are welcome at weekends. Telephone: (39-141) 822822*

a suitable replacement drink with a much lower alcoholic content. Subsequently, a delegation led by the Soviet Deputy Minister for Food visited Piedmont to find a producer as a partner. Russian scientists had developed a unique, ultrasonic system that could reduce the time it takes to obtain the extracts that give vermouth its flavor from 40 days to 45 minutes. Tests were undertaken with encouraging results, and in 1962 the full operation began. The Russian partnership continued until the late 1980s, and negotiations are currently underway to consider resuming such production.

Today, after a spell under other ownership, Riccadonna is back in the hands of another Ottavio Riccadonna, the grandson of the founder. The company still produces Extra Dry White, Bianco (medium-sweet white), and Rosso vermouths. A small volume of Vermouth a l'Orange is also produced for the Italian market.

TO SERVE

Riccadonna vermouth styles are light and elegant, with gentle, delicate perfumes. It is possible that the unique ultrasonic equipment is responsible for its subtle fragrance. Subsequently, they are best consumed without the addition of any overpowering mixer.

The different Riccadonna styles are best served as follows:

Riccadonna Extra Dry:

☆ *On ice, with a slice of lemon*

☆ *With tonic and ice*

Riccadonna Bianco:

☆ *On ice, with a slice of lemon*

☆ *With bitter lemon and ice*

Riccadonna Rosso:

☆ *On ice, with a slice of lemon*

☆ *With dry ginger ale and ice*

PRODUCTION

Riccadonna is the least secretive of the vermouth producers in disclosing details of its blend of 40 different herbs and spices, some from alpine pastures and others from exotic locations all

over the world. It does not, of course, divulge the quantities involved. The items vary from hibiscus flowers and rose petals to ginger, nutmeg, cinnamon, saffron, bitter-orange peels, star anise, gentian, and others that are widely used in most vermouth production. The Russian-designed ultrasonic system, which has now been further modernized, remains its exclusive specialty, and the company blends the concentrates obtained with the most neutral wines available from Puglia and Sicily. Should any of these have offending flavors that might clash with the aromas from the herbs and spices, bentonite is used to fine the wines by gravity. As with other vermouth, fortification is carried out by the addition of neutral alcohol.

Modern facilities for extracting aromatic substances
at the Riccadonna plant

ROSSO ANTICO

Red and Precious

The Italian aperitivo Rosso Antico, which translates literally as Ancient Red, could – with some justification – be more properly called New Red, for in 1974, its owners, the Buton company from Bologna, slightly modified its formula to suit modern consumers. The color, though, didn't change, and Rosso Antico has maintained its characteristic, ruby-red hue.

The aperitif's widespread success across Europe during the 1970s was reflected in its choice of non-Italian celebrities to promote the brand during that time. The French actor Fernandel and singer Charles Aznavour were associated with Rosso Antico. The brand cultivated a sophisticated image and was proud of its association with internationally known artists, such as Pietro Annigoni and Salvador

 KEY FACTS

COMPOSITION	*Various wines, a secret recipe of herbs and spices, and neutral-grape alcohol*
COUNTRY OF ORIGIN	*Italy*
WHERE PRODUCED	*The Buton Distillery, Bologna, Italy*
WORLDWIDE ANNUAL SALES VOLUME	*2.4 million bottles*
PRIME MARKETS	*Greece, Australia, and Belgium*

Dalì. Annigoni was comm-issioned to create his own version of the typical Rosso Antico *coppa* (glass), while Dalì designed three of its bottles.

PRODUCTION

Rosso Antico is an aromatized wine that is lightly fortified. It is made from a blend of five base wines, of which Ancellotta Rosso from the Reggio Emilia vineyards is perhaps the most important, since it influences the balance of the drink's rich-red color. This blend accounts for 75 percent of the final volume and to it is added a secret recipe of 32 herbs and spices including sage, thyme, rosemary, elder, china bark, and Chinese rhubarb. The extracts are obtained both by maceration in a neutral-grape alcohol and infusion. Bitter and sweet orange peels predominate.

TO SERVE

Rosso Antico has a bright, ruby-red color and a distinctive herby aroma, with some notes of citrus and vanilla. It is well-balanced on the palate, with a bittersweet taste and pleasant aftertaste of peels and spices.

Traditionally, Rosso Antico can be served as follows:

☆ Coat the rim of the glass with sugar, fill the glass with ice, pour the aperitif over the ice, and finally, add a slice of orange, or lemon if preferred. (The latter is particularly recommended for those with a sweet tooth, as it encourages the bittersweet effect.)

☆ On ice, with a slice of orange

A slice of orange or lemon enhances the flavor of Rosso Antico

St.RAPHAËL

The Soldiers and the Saint

Throughout its 150 years of existence, St. Raphaël has always been the major rival of Dubonnet. Both aperitifs were created in the 1840s as quinine-based aromatized wines for the medicinal purpose of protecting French troops in North Africa against malaria. Joseph Dubonnet and Alphonse Juppet, the creator of St. Raphaël, competed in Paris to be the first to supply the French government with such a drink, and it was Dubonnet who won the race. Juppet had sustained permanent damage to his eyesight while he experimented to find his ideal recipe of herbs and spices for disguising the bitterness of quinine. In his desperation to finish his task, Juppet prayed to St. Raphaël, the patron of good health, that his sight might survive until his work had reached completion. The prayer was answered, and in thanksgiving, Alphonse Juppet named his drink St. Raphaël.

PRODUCTION

Little is known about St. Raphaël's production, except that a secret recipe of herbs and spices, which does not include worm-

KEY FACTS

COMPOSITION	A secret recipe of herbs and spices, wine, and neutral alcohol
COUNTRY OF ORIGIN	France
WHERE PRODUCED	Paris, France
PRIME MARKETS	France

wood, is used. Their extracts are then blended with white wine for St. Raphaël Ambré and red wine for St. Raphaël Rouge. A *mistelle* is also added.

A 1939 *poster advertising* St. Raphaël *Quinquina*

TO SERVE

St. Raphaël Ambré *has a pale-gold color and an elegant bouquet, in which traces of floral notes can be detected. The taste of peels is noticeable on the palate, and it has a slightly sweet, herby aftertaste.*

St. Raphaël Rouge *has a dark, red-wine color and a pungent bouquet. It is tangy and full on the palate, and has a distinctively herby aftertaste.*

Both drinks may be served as follows:

☆ *Chilled, with a slice of lemon or orange*

☆ *On ice, with a slice of lemon or orange*

☆ *On ice, with bitter lemon* (St. Raphaël Rouge *only*)

☆ *With tonic, soda, or Seven Up/Sprite to taste*

SUZE

Suzanne's Favorite Drink

Although Suze was officially launched as a brand in 1889, its origins can be traced as far back as 1795. Fernand Moureaux, the creator of Suze, wanted to make a drink that was beneficial to health, but not wine-based like the majority of aperitifs. He felt that wine quality was too unreliable, since it varied from year to year. He therefore created Suze, a gentian-based aperitif. The origins of the name "Suze" are less clear, however.

Suze is said to come from Fernand Moureaux's sister-in-law, Suzanne, who was known as "Suze" and whose favorite aperitif was "une gentiane." Another more prosaic version is that Moureaux brought the formula for his aperitif - and its name - from Switzerland.

 KEY FACTS

COMPOSITION	Alcohol, water, gentian, other herbs, and sugar
COUNTRY OF ORIGIN	France
WHERE PRODUCED	Créteil, France
WORLDWIDE ANNUAL SALES VOLUME	3,265,700 gallons
PRIME MARKETS	France, Spain, Switzerland, The Benelux Countries
AWARDS	Numerous. Among the most important are medals won in exhibitions in Turin (1911), Paris (1931), and Brussels (1935)
VISITORS	Groups are welcome. Please telephone the Pernod Group at Créteil to make arrangements. Telephone: (33) 149815220

TO SERVE

Suze has a clear, amber-gold color and a complex, herby bouquet. It is rich and luscious on the palate, with a distinctive, long, tangy, dry after-taste. It is best served as follows:

☆ Straight, on ice, in a wide, heavy-bottomed tumbler

☆ One-third Suze to two-thirds orange juice, on ice, in a tall, heavy-bottomed glass

☆ One-third Suze to two-thirds tonic, on ice, in a tall, heavy-bottomed glass

Harvesting gentian roots with the "devil's fork"

Suze is the definitive gentian-flavored aperitif. Although other aromatic plants are used in its production, *Gentiana lutea* is the principal ingredient in this spirit-based drink. Sometimes called "yellow gentian" due to the color of its flowers, the plant takes its name from King Gentius of Illyria, who lived in 172 B.C. and who was the first to recognize gentian's medicinal properties.

PRODUCTION

Gentian grows in the hills of the Jura and Auvergne regions, and it is the roots that are used to make the base for the drink. The roots are harvested in the fall, and are so tenacious that a special fork with two long prongs, known as a "devil's fork," is used to prise them from the soil. They are then washed and taken to the factory at Créteil, where they are sorted, and chopped roughly, ready for maceration (steeping) in alcohol. After three to four years, the gentian-flavored alcohol is distilled twice, and is then blended with other herbs that have also been macerated. A final filtration ensures purity and clarity of color.

WARNINKS ADVOCAAT

The Aperitif from Amsterdam

The company of Erven Warnink was established in Amsterdam in 1616, when production was very labor-intensive. Since its move in 1974 to an ultramodern plant at Middelharnis, in southwest Holland, it has only 35 employees, yet much of the traditional process is retained. The plant has a capacity of 10 million bottles per annum, and is the largest producer of advocaat in The Netherlands.

The word "advocaat" is generally considered to be a corruption of the Brazilian word "avocado," the indigenous fruit that was used by the early Portuguese colonists to make an alcoholic drink. Later, this custom was adopted by Dutch sailors after returning to their native country from voyages to South America. They began to produce an "advocaat" in their own style. To this day, it remains a mystery why they selected egg yolks, rather than the avocado pears used by the Portuguese settlers.

Earlier this century, advocaat was often used by professional sports teams as a restorative drink.

KEY FACTS

COMPOSITION	Alcohol, egg yolks, sugar, and flavorings
COUNTRY OF ORIGIN	The Netherlands
WHERE PRODUCED	Middelharnis, southwest Holland
PRIME MARKETS	The Netherlands, UK, Germany, Norway

TO SERVE

The bright yellow, opaque color of **Warninks Advocaat** *is its most distinctive feature; that and its thick, creamy texture make it instantly recognizable.*

Serve it as follows:

☆ *Chilled, on its own in a liqueur glass*

☆ *Tall, on ice with Seven Up/Sprite*

☆ *With dry sherry on a cold winter's day*

PRODUCTION

Warninks Advocaat has an abv of 17.2 percent and is made with a neutral-spirit base. Its prime ingredient is fresh egg yolks, but the identity of the others is confidential. The eggs come from farms where hygiene and nutrition are carefully monitored; these are brought to the cellars when only three days old, and subjected to rigorous examination for quality at the production plant. Production normally takes seven weeks from start to finish.

The old Warnink factory in Amsterdam

129

PART THREE

THE GENERIC
DIRECTORY

CREME DE CASSIS

The Canon's Recipe

This is one of the most unorthodox claimants to the name *aperitif*, because crème de cassis, a blackcurrant liqueur, does not, strictly speaking, fall within any of the defined aperitif categories. However, it is an essential component in one of France's best-known aperitifs, Kir.

The original recipe for crème de cassis was devised by Denis Lagoute in 1841, in the French region of Dijon. Lejay-Lagoute is still widely regarded as the classic brand of crème de cassis, with Sisca and Marie Brizard being other popular labels.

Crème de cassis had been enjoyed as an afterdinner liqueur for a number of generations, before a surprising intervention gave it a new role. The man responsible was Canon Felix Kir, a courageous leader of both local government and the French Resistance during the Second World War. He began mixing his local liqueur with chilled, dry white wine, thus creating the aperitif that became known as Kir. When mixed with sparkling wine or champagne, it is given the grander title of Kir Royal.

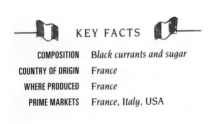

KEY FACTS

COMPOSITION	Black currants and sugar
COUNTRY OF ORIGIN	France
WHERE PRODUCED	France
PRIME MARKETS	France, Italy, USA

TO SERVE

Kir: *Pour one part crème de cassis into a tall, narrow wine glass. Add five parts of dry white wine.*

Kir Royal: *One part crème de cassis to five parts dry, white, sparkling wine or champagne, served in a champagne flute.*

For a luxurious touch, add a few black currants preserved in crème de cassis.

PRODUCTION

Only the ripest, finest black currants are picked for pressing, and their pulp is poured into giant oak vats to be macerated in neutral alcohol. When several months have elapsed, the liquid is drawn off, and a sugar solution is added. The resulting liqueur is then filtered and bottled. No artificial coloring is permitted.

Champagne – or sparkling wine – is one of the components of Kir Royal

FRENCH VINS DOUX NATURELS

The Southern French Tradition

The main fortified wines that come under this category are Banyuls, Rivesaltes, and Maury, all from the Bas-Pyrenées region, and rasteau from the southern Rhône region. The principal grape variety used is Grenache, but

Banyuls vineyards

this can be supplemented by Macabeo, Malvoisie, Muscat d'Alexandria, Carignan, Cinsault, and Syrah grapes.

The region of the Bas-Pyrenées was first planted with vines by the Romans, but in the aftermath of a Moorish invasion in 717 A.D., viticulture was discouraged. Later, when Charlemagne defeated the Moors in 801 A.D., he made the area part of his great empire, actively encouraging the production of wine there.

BANYULS

The beautiful vineyards of Banyuls are situated on the French coast near Perpignan, not far from the border with Spain, and the grapes derive a certain freshness from their proximity to the sea. In many ways, some of the Banyuls' characteristics reflect those of certain styles of port. Banyuls is often sold at five or ten years of age, and some exceptional, older styles exist, like Castell des Hospices Banyuls Grand Cru 1982, which is aged in oak for seven years and in bottles for eight or more. Another popular label is Banyuls Rimage Cuvée Regis Boucabeille 1989. Banyuls is drunk both as an aperitif and as a dessert wine.

Banyuls is a *vin cuit*, or cooked wine, like Noilly Prat, made in *blanc*, *doré*, and *rouge* styles. The Grenache Blanc grape variety is used for the *blanc* and *doré* styles, and the Grenache Rouge for the *rouge.* The grapes for the *blanc* are pressed very lightly and fermented in stainless-steel, temperature-controlled vats. The next stage is to fortify the new wine with neutral-grape brandy, after which it is bottled and cellared for 18 months. Both the *doré* and the *rouge* are aged outdoors for 12 months in small, oak casks called *demi-muids*, and later in glass demi-johns, where they are subjected to all the vicissitudes of the elements. This procedure is acknowledged as speeding up the maturation of the wines. The *doré* is basically a *blanc* that has been left to age outdoors in the same manner as the *rouge*. Both these styles are then returned to the cellars, where they are separately blended in large, oak vats, and then allowed to marry before being bottled. Further bottle aging takes place before they are ready for marketing. The minimum age for releasing a Banyuls is 18 months.

MAURY

Maury is quite similar to Banyuls. Among the best-known brands are Mas Amiel and D'Ogival.

Maury is a *vin cuit*, and the new wine is placed outdoors for 12 months in giant, glass bottles called *"bon-bons."* Here, the wine experiences all the daily changes of temperature, humidity, and atmospheric pressure. Afterwards, it is transferred to cellars and aged for a further period of four to nine years, depending on whether it will be sold at five or ten years of age.

RASTEAU

Rasteau is made in a similar style to Banyuls, but is not aged outdoors. Instead, it is aged in small, oak barrels, usually for five or more years. The foremost producer is Emile Bressy.

RIVESALTES

Rivesaltes is a close neighbor of Banyuls, and should not be confused with Muscat de Rivesaltes (see muscat section). Only red styles are produced; Chateau Valmy is one of the best examples.

The production of Rivesaltes is very similar to that of Banyuls.

BANYULS RIMAGE
CUVÉE REGIS BOUCABEILLE
1989

Aged by the Elements

The Cuvée Regis Boucabeille is an outstanding example of a mature Banyuls made from 90 percent Grenache Noir and 10 percent Carignan, both of which are red-grape varieties. It is exposed to the elements for a shorter period of time than many other Banyuls, and is bottled in the spring following the vintage. After bottling, it is aged underground until ready for shipment.

TO SERVE

Cuvée Regis Boucabeille has a mature, deep-red color, a full, vinous bouquet, and is full and rich on the palate, with a lingering, slightly sweet aftertaste. It is best served as follows:

☆ *Cellar-cool, in a port glass*

 KEY FACTS

COMPOSITION	Red wine and neutral-grape brandy
COUNTRY OF ORIGIN	France
WHERE PRODUCED	Cave Cooperative, Banyuls, France
WORLDWIDE ANNUAL SALES VOLUME	1,339,200 bottles
PRIME MARKETS	France, Belgium, The Netherlands, Luxembourg, Germany
VISITORS	Trade visitors only. Telephone: (33) 468880322

MAURY VINCENT
D'OGIVAL

The Wine from the French Pyrenées

This is a typical Maury, which can be consumed both as an aperitif or as an accompaniment to dessert or cheese courses. It is made from 100 percent Grenache Noir grapes that are grown on the slopes of a small valley in the French Pyrenées, in the 4,375 acres of the official *appellation contrôlée* region of Maury.

The first stage of the six-year-long production period is to take the free-run juice that comes from the newly-picked grapes. This juice gives a must that remains in contact with the grape skins during a longer-than-usual fermentation period of 20 days. The wine is then fortified with neutral-grape brandy before the grapes are pressed for the second time. The resulting liquid is left to settle in concrete vats for six months. Afterwards, the wine is drawn off into large, glass *bon-bons* (20-gallon-capacity, lollipop-shaped bottles) and left outdoors to age for one year. Following this, the contents are transferred to the main aging cellar, where

KEY FACTS

COMPOSITION	*Red wine and neutral-grape brandy*
COUNTRY OF ORIGIN	*France*
WHERE PRODUCED	*Maury, Bas-Pyrenées, France*
WORLDWIDE ANNUAL SALES VOLUME	*1.3 million bottles*
PRIME MARKET	*France*

TO SERVE

Maury Vincent D'Ogival has an amber hue, and a bouquet with hints of coffee. It is very supple, fairly full-bodied and rich on the palate, with some noticeable tannins, and has a long well-balanced finish. It is best served as follows:

☆ At room temperature, in small port or similar glasses

the wine matures in large, oak casks of about 8,000 gallons for a further four years, before being filtered and finally bottled. The wine undergoes a further six months' bottle aging before being released for sale.

Banyuls vineyards with the Château de Queribus in the distance

MADEIRA

Historic Drink from a Perfect Climate

Madeira is a fortified wine that comes from the rocky island of the same name, located some 400 miles in the Atlantic Ocean, west of Morocco. Madeira has one of the most consistent climates in the world, with an average daily temperature of around 70°F. Virtually every morning, its 6,000-foot mountain peak is obscured by clouds that drop their rain on the summit. This water runs by gravity down to the vineyards through a network of channels known as *levadas*.

Vineyards were first planted in Madeira early in the fifteenth century, A.D. When Alvise da Mosto, a Venetian explorer, landed on the island in 1455, he sent back reports that "the vines of Madeira are the finest sight in the world." As early as the sixteenth century, Madeira wine was shipped to the British Isles, France, and The Netherlands, and was first shipped to the Americas in 1567. At that time, Madeira was not fortified, and it was always shipped in casks, usually being sold under the name of the grape variety used, such as Malvasia, Malmsey, or Terrantez.

Madeira was just becoming established in northern Europe when the shipping came to an abrupt halt when the Spanish

Madeira is aged in special ground-floor cellars

occupied the island from 1580 to 1665. During that period, the production of a wine that competed with several others from the Spanish mainland was discouraged, and the island was largely planted with sugar cane.

Nonetheless, some wine production continued, and it was probably during the Spanish occupation that the solera system, as practiced in the sherry region of Spain, was adopted, as was fortification. However, the solera system had one drawback on Madeira's ancient, volcanic rock: it required a lot of cellar space, which was not readily available on the steeply terraced, hillside vineyards of Madeira. The wine producers solved this problem by adapting the solera method on a smaller, finer scale, making soleras that used wine from exceptional vintages only, and still on a very small scale. The results were some magnificent old soleras, which can still occasionally be found at auctions.

PRODUCTION

Today, there are some 4,000 small growers on Madeira supplying many of the houses. For centuries, the grapes were pressed by treading, but these days, virtually all of the grapes are crushed in pneumatic presses. Madeira, in keeping with many other wines produced on the Iberian peninsula, is fortified by adding young, neutral-grape brandy to the new white wine. However, it boasts a unique "cooking" process, which influences its style, known as an *estufagem*. Originally, this involved aging the wine in demi-johns and barrels in the roof spaces above the cellars. The temperature changes speeded up the maturation of the wines in a process similar to that of a French *vin cuit*. Nowadays, the old-style *estufagems* have been replaced by special ground-floor cellars.

MADEIRA STYLES

Not all Madeiras can claim to be aperitifs. Sercial, the driest style, and Verdelho, a medium-dry, are both named after their grape varieties, and are ideal served chilled or cellar-cool as aperitifs. The rich, sweeter styles are better with desserts.

BLANDY's

The Officer Turned Winemaker

Of the British-owned brands of Madeira, Blandy's is the best-known name. The house was founded in 1811 by John Blandy, who served as an officer in the British garrison that was sent to the island at the request of the Portuguese in 1807, as they feared an invasion by Napoleonic forces. Ironically, the only occasion on which Napoleon saw Madeira was on his way to his final exile in St. Helena. But John Blandy had fallen in love with the island and its wines, and had decided to sell his estate in England and come to live in Madeira. He developed a business in Funchal, comprising his own wine cellars, a shipping business, and later, even a bank!

The winemaking process begins in August with the picking of the grape varieties needed for the drier styles, such as Sercial and Verdelho, and concludes in November with Malmsey, the sweetest.

 KEY FACTS

COMPOSITION	Wine and neutral grape brandy
COUNTRY OF ORIGIN	Portugal
WHERE PRODUCED	Funchal, Madeira, Portugal
PRIME MARKETS	UK, France, Belgium, Germany
AWARDS	A Gold Medal in the 1995 International Wine Challenge, London
VISITORS	Welcome at the Madeira Wine Association, Funchal. Telephone: (351-91) 740 110

TO SERVE

Blandy's Duke of Sussex has a golden hue, a slightly oaky nose, is firm and quite full on the palate with a pleasant dry finish.

Blandy's Five-Year-Old Sercial is a pale-rust color, with a nose reminiscent of apples. It has a pleasing freshness, balanced with a soft, nutty maturity.

Blandy's Five-Year-Old Verdelho has a red-gold color, a slightly smoky aroma, a flavor of dried fruit, and a slightly sweet, lingering aftertaste.

All three styles should be served as follows:

☆ *Well chilled, in a copita or tulip-shaped glass, with nuts or tapas*

For generations, Blandy's persisted with the traditional method of treading grapes in granite tanks or *lagares*, but they have recently converted to the most modern, automatic presses. From these presses, the juice runs into large, temperature-controlled, stainless-steel vats. The new wines are then fortified with neutral-grape brandy at different stages of their fermentation.

The Madeira Wine Institute monitors standards

HENRIQUES &
HENRIQUES

The Largest Independent Producer

The Henriques family can trace their genealogy back to 1094 A.D., when the Burgundian Comte Henri arrived on mainland Portugal. Since the fifteenth century, they have been the largest landowners in the Camara de Lobos area of Madeira. It was here that the Portuguese explorer, Zarco the Squint-eyed, planted the first vines between 1420 and 1425 on land that the family still own. Today, Henriques & Henriques own the most modern, major vineyard on the island of Madeira, which was also the first to be mechanized. The 25-acre vineyard was planted in 1995 at Quinta

KEY FACTS

COMPOSITION	*Wine and neutral-grape brandy*
COUNTRY OF ORIGIN	*Portugal*
WHERE PRODUCED	*The island of Madeira, off the coast of northwest Africa*
WORLDWIDE ANNUAL SALES VOLUME	*800,000 bottles*
PRIME MARKETS	*Germany, Sweden, and France*
AWARDS	*A 1943 Antwerp award and success in the 1997 Asia-Pacific Wine Challenge*
VISITORS	*Welcome by prior appointment. Telephone: (351-91) 941551*

TO SERVE

3 YEARS OLD

Monte Seco: A light, pale, dry Madeira. It is best served as follows:

★ Chilled
★ On ice
★ As a tall drink, with ice and tonic

Special Dry: A tangy, crisp, refreshingly dry Madeira, with a nutty bouquet.

Medium-dry: An elegant, golden Madeira, which is quite fruity and has a tangy aftertaste.

Both styles are best served well chilled

5 YEARS OLD

Finest Dry: This fine, dry Madeira has a slightly oak-like nose, with a firm, crisp finish.

Finest medium-dry: A gentle, mellow Madeira with some oak in the bouquet. It is quite smooth, and has an attractive, tangy aftertaste.

Both styles are best served well chilled

10 YEARS OLD

Sercial: A classic, dry single-varietal Madeira with a fresh aroma. This middle-weight wine has a complexity that balances spiciness with some acidity, and has a fine, long finish.

Verdelho: The traditional, medium-dry favorite on the island, it is medium-bodied and has a rich-amber color. Its complex aroma and robust character make it a beautifully balanced wine with a long finish.

Both styles are best served chilled

Grande, about half a mile above sea level. Henriques & Henriques is the largest independent producer and shipper of Madeira wines, and the only house that owns vineyards. The company markets its wines at three, five, and ten years of age. They are produced from noble *vinifera* varieties only, such as Sercial, Verdelho, Tinta Negra Mole, and Listrão.

The harvesting of the grapes begins in August, and lasts until November. During this period, the five approved Madeira varieties – Sercial, Verdelho, Bual, Malmsey, and Tinta Negra – are picked. The first four are white grapes that have their skins separated from the must when pressed. Conversely, with the Tinta Negra, a little skin contact is allowed, but great care is taken to ensure that during the pressing, no red color runs into the must. The new wines are then fortified with neutral grape brandy before being aged in an *estufagem* and finally, in bottles.

MALAGA

Wine from the Hills

The city of Malaga in the province of Andalusia lies on the Mediterranean coast of Spain, just northeast of Gibraltar. Inland, to the north and east of the city, the hills rise steeply, and it is on these hillside slopes that the best vines are grown. Hence, the old term for Malaga of "mountain wine." Malaga has a very long history of viticulture, and over the centuries has suffered successive invasions by Phoenician, Greeks, Carthaginians, and, most importantly perhaps, the Romans. Toward the end of the third century, B.C., Malaga was one of the first settlements along the Spanish Mediterranean coast to fall to the invading Roman forces, who are generally believed to have established organized viticulture in the area.

A Malaga bar

On the slopes to the north of Malaga, which rise to some 1,625 feet above sea level, the main vine variety is Pedro Ximenez, while moscatel vines dominate the eastern slopes. These are the two leading grape varieties approved by the *Consejo Regulador*, the official body that determines which wines qualify for the *Malaga Denominacion de Origen*. Wines must also be matured in the city of Malaga itself. Malaga wines range from very sweet to dry, and while most are a blend of moscatel and Pedro Ximenez, some are made exclusively from a single varietal. Additionally, their alcohol content varies between 15° and 23°, as they are sometimes lightly fortified with neutral-grape alcohol. The main Malaga styles are *lagrima* (tears), *dulce* (sweet), *semi-dulce* (semi-sweet), and *blanco seco* (dry). The sweetest and darkest Malagas are usually drunk as accompaniments to desserts, and these are at their best when served at room temperature. The medium and dry styles make delightful aperitifs if drunk chilled. Among the foremost producers are Scholtz Hermanos and Lopez Hermanos.

PRODUCTION

Lagrima is made from the free-run juice that is squeezed out of the grapes naturally, under the pressure of their own weight, when the bunches are piled on top of one another at harvest time. This juice is collected and then made into a delightfully luscious and sweet wine. The other styles are made by pressing the grapes mechanically. Once the grapes are pressed, the juice is fermented in large, cylindrical, cement vessels, similar to the *tinajas* of Montilla. The new wine is then transported in tankers to Malaga, where it is stored in wooden vats prior to blending. The blend varies depending on the style of the final product. A number of permitted sweetening agents may be used in the blend to give it color and flavor. The most important is *arrope* (syrup), made by boiling the unfermented grape juice in a copper pan until it becomes a dark, molasses-like substance that tastes a little like burnt sugar. The majority of Malaga is aged with the same solera system used in Jerez, but using six scales of American-oak butts.

LOPEZ HERMANOS
MALAGA VIRGEN

The Brothers' Sweet Wine

Lopez Hermanos was founded in the late-nineteenth century by Don Salvador Lopez Lopez who with his brother erected the first cellars in Cruz del Molinillo in 1896.

Lopez Hermanos Malaga Virgen is made from a blend of Pedro Ximenez and moscatel grapes. Lopez Hermanos Malaga Virgen is aged for two years in wooden barrels before it is ready to be bottled for marketing.

TO SERVE

Lopez Hermanos Malaga Virgen is clear and brilliant, with an old-gold hue. It has a vinous bouquet, is sweet and unctuous on the palate; has yeasty undertones, and a lingering, slightly caramelized aftertaste. It is best served as follows:

☆ Cellar cool, in a port glass

☆ At room temperature, in a port glass

  ## KEY FACTS

COMPOSITION	Pedro Ximenez and moscatel grapes, plus neutral-grape brandy
COUNTRY OF ORIGIN	Spain
WHERE PRODUCED	Malaga, Spain
VISITORS	Visitors are welcome at the winery at Canada 10, 29006 Malaga, Spain, from Monday to Friday between 9:30 a.m. to 2:00 p.m. (Note: the winery is closed in August.) Telephone: (34-5) 2319454

MARSALA

The Toast of Trafalgar

The first vineyards were planted by Greek settlers at Marsala on the island of Sicily, Italy, in the seventh century, B.C. As was their usual practice in their Mediterranean colonies, they brought vine cuttings with them from their homeland. The town's name is said to be derived from the Roman general Claudius Marcellus, who was apparently given a vineyard in the area as a reward for defeating the enemy at the Battle of Syracuse.

The Greek colonists produced still table-wines only, and that continued to be the case until the late-eighteenth century, when a young English merchant, John Woodhouse, began fortifying the local wine in an effort to emulate sherry. He was followed by another Englishman, Benjamin Ingham, who founded a rival

The Florio Marsala cellars

house. Between them, they developed a thriving trade throughout the British Empire. In 1833, the first major Sicilian wine producer, Vincenzo Florio, successfully targeted the North American market, making Marsala a truly international wine.

The most famous Marsala producer was Admiral Horatio Nelson, who was given a vineyard there by Ferdinand, King of the Two Sicilies, as a reward for protecting the royal family against the Napoleonic forces. Nelson showed his business acumen when he persuaded the British government that the Navy should use his Marsala for the victory toast. The result was an order for 500 pipes, the equivalent of 282,000 bottles, per annum. The story ended ironically, however, for when the British Navy defeated the French at Trafalgar in 1805, the British sailors were saluting their admiral with his own Marsala, not realizing that at that very moment, he lay dying on the deck of his flagship, the H.M.S. Victory.

PRODUCTION

Marsala is a fortified wine produced in vineyards surrounding the ancient port of Marsala, in the Trapani province on the west coast of Sicily. It is vinified in *oro* (gold), red, and ruby styles, and is marketed at various ages, from two years upwards, with an occasional, single-vintage of around 30 years old. There is also a style of Marsala known as "Vergine," which is made without using any *mistelle* or cooking must.

The chief grape varieties used are Grillo and Cataratto, and the best vineyards are those that reach right down to the water's edge, as the cool, coastal breezes help the grapes to retain a good acid balance. Until recent years, the vines had always been trained close to the ground, but research by the house of Carlo Pellegrino led to the conclusion that training them on trellises produced healthier fruit. Most Marsala is made by pressing these two grape varieties, fortifying them with neutral-grape brandy, and then blending them with a *mistelle* and cooking must; some Marsalas are also aged and blended using a solera system, but not all are produced in this manner.

FLORIO TERRE ARSE
MARSALA VERGINE 1986

The Leading Marsala in the USA

I n 1833, Vincenzo Florio, a prominent shipper and merchant, decided that it was about time a Sicilian should be the leader in the production of Marsala rather than a Briton.

He noticed that on the waterfront, between the two English-owned houses of Woodhouse and Ingham, there was a large plot of undeveloped land. He purchased it, and from this vantage point could spy on the opposition, gleaning sufficient information about their pricing policies and key markets to plan his own strategy. There was little point in competing

 KEY FACTS

COMPOSITION	Wine and grape alcohol
COUNTRY OF ORIGIN	Italy
WHERE PRODUCED	The west coast of Sicily, Italy
WORLDWIDE ANNUAL SALES VOLUME	700,000 bottles
PRIME MARKETS	USA, Japan, Germany
AWARDS	Gold Medals in 1994 and 1997, at the International Wine Competition in Verona, Italy
VISITORS	Visitors are welcome to the winery, cellars, and Florio wine museum by prior appointment. Opening times: Monday through Thursday, from 9:30 a.m. to 11:30 a.m. and 3:00 p.m. to 4:30 p.m. Fridays from 9:00 a.m. to 12 noon. Telephone: (39-11) 6300737

with them in the British market, and so Florio decided to target the eastern seaboard of the United Stages, where the British were still out of favor after the Revolutionary War. Making use of his extensive shipping fleet, the house of Florio soon established a flourishing trade in America, and his label is still the leading Marsala brand in the U.S., more than a century and a half later. Florio Terre Arse Marsala Vergine 1986 comes from the 1986 vintage, and is distinguished by being completely unblended.

> ## TO SERVE
>
> Terra Arse Marsala Vergine 1986 has a burnished, old-gold color, and an elegant nose, with hints of toasted almonds and honey. It is smooth and slightly sweet on the palate, with a long finish. As it becomes warmer, its aroma and flavor develop.
> Like all single-vintage Marsala, it should be served as follows:
>
> ☆ Sipped, at cellar temperature, from a small glass similar to a port glass

Florio Terre Arse Marsala Vergine 1986 does not contain any *mistelle* or cooking must, and was simply fortified with young grape alcohol at the time of pressing. It spent approximately eight years aging in oak casks, and a further six months aging in bottles prior to marketing.

Florio workers outside the company's cellars (c. 1900)

PELLEGRINO GARIBALDI
MARSALA

Garibaldi's Favorite

Pellegrino is by far the most successful of all the Marsala producers. Founded in 1880, it is still an independent, family-operated business, and is responsible for nearly 80 percent of all Marsala production. Its cellars are situated in the ancient city of Marsala, in the Trapani province on the west coast of Sicily.

Up to the eighteenth century, Marsala was a fairly ordinary table wine, until the British shipper John Woodhouse introduced fortification, which enabled the drink to survive long journeys. Soon, new markets were established, both in northern Europe, and a little later, in the United States. He also developed the use of the solera system for some styles of Marsala, based on his knowledge of sherry production. Pellegrino Garibaldi Marsala is the company's most popular style, and is rich,

 KEY FACTS

COMPOSITION	DOC wine, neutral alcohol, mistelle, and cooking must
COUNTRY OF ORIGIN	Italy
WHERE PRODUCED	Marsala, Sicily, Italy
WORLDWIDE ANNUAL SALES VOLUME	18 million bottles
PRIME MARKETS	Italy, U.K., France, and USA
VISITORS	Visitors welcome: Telephone: (39-923) 951177

> ## TO SERVE
>
> P*ellegrino Garibaldi Marsala is a deep, nut-brown color with a vinous nose. It has a rich, sweet, full flavor that lingers on the palate.*
>
> *It is best served as follows:*
>
> ☆ *On its own, well chilled*
>
> ☆ *With ice*

sweet, and very smooth. It takes its name from the Italian patriot Garibaldi, whose army first landed at Marsala in 1860, with the intention of unifying Italy. Legend has it that Garibaldi liked to sit in the evening sun and sip this particular style of the drink.

The grapes pressed for Pellegrino Garibaldi Marsala are the Grillo and Cataratto varieties from the family's 1,000 acres of the official, Marsala-denominated vineyards. The grapes are crushed at a cellar in the vineyards to retain their freshness. Afterwards, they are transported to the main Pellegrino cellar in the town of Marsala, where other items, such as neutral alcohol, a *mistelle*, and cooking must, are added; Garibaldi Marsala is then aged for around four years in large, oak vats.

A limited volume of Marsala for some of the other styles is still made using a solera system.

Pellegrino's Tenuta San Nicola vineyard estate

MONTILLA

The Hottest Vineyards in Europe

The official D.O.C. wine region of Montilla-Moriles lies just south of Cordoba, in the Spanish province of Andalusia. The vineyards are planted on white, chalky limestone soil between three rivers, the Guadalquivir, Guadajoz, and Genil. Unlike the Jerez region, where three different grape varieties are permitted, only Pedro Ximenez vines are cultivated here.

As this is an inland region, it was never settled by the Greeks, as were the coastal regions of Spain. The first vineyards were planted by the Romans toward the end of the third century B.C. Also, unlike Jerez or Oporto, there has never been a British tradition here.

The word "amontillado" originated in Montilla, and was used to designate a wine made in its style. Other regions annexed the term to describe medium-dry styles, as in nearby Jerez, where

A vineyard in the Montilla region

153

The classic tinajas receive the must, once fermentation is over

many sherries are called "amontillado." The difference between amontillado in Montilla and elsewhere is that in other regions, the style is fortified, whereas genuine Montilla is not. The Montilla-Moriles denomination area makes *finos*, *olorosos*, and sweet styles of Montilla. Among the best-known Montilla producers are Club Royal and Perez Barquero.

PRODUCTION

After a cool spring, summer temperatures soar, and the sun bakes the earth, making Montilla one of the hottest vine-yard climates in Europe. As a result, the Pedro Ximenez grapes ripen to such a degree that it is unnecessary to fortify the wine. The juice reaches an alcohol level of 14.5 to 15 percent quite naturally, as a result of fermenting in giant, earthenware jars called *tinajas*.

GRAN BARQUERO
FINO MONTILLA

A Leader in its Field

Perez Barquero S.A. has been marketing Montilla since 1906, and today is a recognized leader in the field. Three ranges of Montilla, namely Los Palcos, Los Amigos, and Gran Barquero, are made by the company, and each range includes various Montilla styles, such as *fino*, *amontillado*, medium, pale-cream, and *oloroso*. The main wines shipped are under the Los Amigos (three-year-old Montilla) and Gran Barquero (15- to 20-year-old) labels.

Only Pedro Ximenez grapes are used to make Gran Barquero Fino Montilla. After crushing, Perez Barquero use modern, stainless-steel vats for the fermentation, but then separate the young wine from the lees and transfer it

 KEY FACTS

COMPOSITION	*White wine, made only from 100 percent Pedro Ximenez grapes, unfortified*
COUNTRY OF ORIGIN	*Spain*
WHERE PRODUCED	*Montilla-Moriles, Cordoba, Spain*
WORLDWIDE ANNUAL SALES VOLUME	*Approximately one million bottles*
PRIME MARKETS	*UK, Netherlands, and Belgium*
AWARDS	*A Gold Medal at Seville in 1986; also, Gold, Silver, and Bronze Medals at Vinexpo, Bordeaux, France 1991*
VISITORS	*By prior appointment only. Telephone: (34-57) 650500*

into *tinajas*, or large earthenware jars. At this stage, some of the young wines will develop *flor* and become *finos*; others will not develop *flor*, but will become darker and fuller, and so be classified as *olorosos*, in a pattern similar to that observed in sherry production. The wines are then aged and blended in a solera system. Gran Barquero Fino is arguably the company's top-rated wine; it is blended from *finos* between 5

The cellar-master checks the wines at all stages of production

and 12 years of age, which are then allowed to settle before they are filtered and bottled. One crucial difference between Montilla and its neighbors, Malaga and sherry, is that it is unfortified..

The bodega's "sacristy" where the oldest wines are stored

TO SERVE

Gran Barquero Fino has a bright straw color and a pungent bouquet. It is crisp and dry on the palate, with a fine, lingering aftertaste. It should be served as follows:

☆ Chilled, in a copita

It is ideal on its own, or as an accompaniment to small appetizers or tapas.

MUSCATS

The Fragrant Aroma of the South

The term "muscats" is used in this book to identify those fortified wines made from one of the many muscat grape varieties, such as muscat, muscatel or moscatel. The best-known of the muscat varieties is the Muscat d'Alexandria whose very name betrays its Greek origin. The Greeks cultivated these vines on the islands of the Aegean Sea as early as 800 or 900 B.C. They were later taken by Greek colonists to new settlements scattered around the Mediterranean. The variety had particular appeal because muscat grapes are successful both as dessert grapes and for winemaking.

Muscat grapes

The heady, scented aroma and lusciously sweet taste of muscats means that they are widely enjoyed both as aperitifs and as accompaniments to desserts. Interestingly, they are not always consumed chilled, especially in parts of Italy, where they may be served at room temperature.

On the Italian island of Pantelleria, to the south of Sicily, two muscat wines are produced from the same variety, namely Moscato di Pantelleria and Passito di Pantelleria. The first is a light-golden wine with an elegant balance of flavor, while the Passito has a denser, deep-golden colour, and a bigger, fuller flavor. The best-known name is Pellegrino Passito di Pantelleria.

In France another cousin of the Muscat of Alexandria, the Muscat à Petits Grains, is quite widely used. In some regions, the Muscat of Alexandria is blended with the Muscat à Petits Grains to produce *appellation contrôlée* wines, such as Beaumes-de-Venise,

Frontignan, Rivesaltes and Lunel. Of these, Muscat de Beaumes-de-Venise is found in many international markets and may be drunk well chilled as an aperitif or as an accompaniment to dessert courses. The Caves de Vignerons and Domaine de Durban both market particularly fine examples of Muscat de Beaumes-de-Venise.

On the eastern Mediterranean coast of Spain, Moscatel de Valencia, which makes a charming and fragrant aperitif, is produced. The most successful label is Castillo de Liria. On the western side of the Iberian peninsula, the most distinctive example is Moscatel de Setubal from near Lisbon, on the Atlantic coast of Portugal.

California is home to a particularly delightful aperitif muscat called Essencia, which is produced by Andrew Quady from Orange Blossom Muscat.

PRODUCTION

The majority of muscats are produced for early consumption, and are not usually aged to any notable degree, with the exception of the Portuguese Moscatel de Setubal. Most muscat grapes are usually picked when ripe or even overripe to ensure that the highest possible grape-sugar level and flavor are obtained. The grapes are crushed with the skins, and the fermentation is carefully monitored by the cellarmaster. At the optimum point, depending on what style of muscat he is making, he adds neutral grape brandy to stop the fermentation. In many instances, this is done when the grape skins are still in contact with the wine, the effect is to extract the finest aromas. Afterward, the wine is blended, filtered and then aged for one or more years in fiberglass, stainless-steel or oak.

MOSCATEL de SETUBAL
JOSE MARIA DA FONSECA

A Unique Wine from Portugal

In much of Europe, any wine marketed as "varietal" – a wine that is identified by the name of the grape variety used – must be produced 100 percent from that specific variety. However, that is not the case with Moscatel de Setubal from Portugal. In 1834, when José Maria da Fonseca began making and shipping his wine, he decided that 70 percent of its blend should be the Moscatel de Setubal variety, and the remaining 30 percent should be made up of four other local varieties: Arinto, Boais, Rabo de Ovelha, and Rupeiro. These non-moscatel grapes give the blend its freshness and acidity. These proportions became the very principle on which the official Moscatel de Setubal denomination was based when it was ratified by law in 1907.

 KEY FACTS

COMPOSITION	Wine, neutral grape brandy, and grape juice
COUNTRY OF ORIGIN	Portugal
WHERE PRODUCED	Setubal, Portugal
WORLDWIDE ANNUAL SALES VOLUME	420,000 bottles
PRIME MARKETS	Portugal, Sweden, Norway, and USA
AWARDS	Gold Medal, Paris, France, 1885
VISITORS	Visitors are welcome. Telephone: (351-1) 219 1500

Grapes have been grown in the region since ancient times

TO SERVE

The younger style, which is normally consumed as an aperitif, has a rich-gold color. Its bouquet is surprisingly fresh and grapey, and provides a fuller flavor. Serve as follows:

☆ Chilled on its own
☆ On ice

By 1850, José Maria was producing his moscatel from vineyards surrounding the Atlantic seaport of Setubal, just south of Lisbon, the Portuguese capital, and exporting it to Brazil, the United States, South Africa, and a number of European countries. A gold medal at the 1885 Paris exhibition further enhanced the wine's excellent reputation.

A unique method of production is involved. The grapes are crushed, and when fermentation is still at a very early stage, neutral-grape brandy is added, both to stop fermentation and to fortify the wine. The wine is then placed in large vats with the skins and pulp of the crushed grapes, and more freshly pressed grapes are added to this blend to give the wine its fragrant, distinctive aroma. After the lees are removed, the wine is transferred to small oak barrels where it ages for a minimum of five years.

The José Maria da Fonseca wine cellars

PEACH-FLAVORED APERITIFS

The Traditional and the International

For many years, drinks producers have tried to make first-rate, peach-flavored aperitifs, but few have succeeded. There are, however, two interesting examples, each of which are quite different in style, and make very unusual aperitifs.

RINQUINQUIN

At Forcalquier, in the Provence region of France, this unusual drink is known as the "seven-peach aperitif," since its manufacture involves the pressing of seven different varieties of peach, as well as infusing their leaves. To these ingredients is added a concentrate of herbs and spices, including china bark (quinine). The resulting liquor is then blended with neutral alcohol and a cane-sugar solution. Rinquinquin is a delightfully fruity aperitif, with several fine, peach flavors, and hints of apricot and vanilla. Peach kernels can be detected in the finish. Rinquinquin should always be served straight, and well chilled.

ARCHERS

Archers was first produced in Canada in 1986. Although it is marketed as a schnapps, it doesn't really match the same description as that used in many European countries. It is a blend of peaches and neutral spirit, and is sold at the unusual level of 23 percent alcohol by volume (abv). Archers can be drunk over ice, with orange juice, tonic, soda water, or Seven Up/Sprite.

PINEAU DES CHARENTES

The Appellation Contrôlée Aperitif

As an aperitif, Pineau des Charentes is unique in that it can only be produced from grapes found in the French *appellation contrôlée* (A.C.) region of Cognac, the region of the world's most distinguished brandy. For centuries, most farmers used Folle Blanche, Ugni Blanc, and Colombard grape varieties for their pineau, but now regulations have been relaxed.

PRODUCTION

The grapes are picked when fully ripe and sweet, and immediately after pressing, a one-year-old cognac is added to the juice to prevent fermentation. This procedure both fortifies the juice, and helps to retain the full flavor and sweetness of the fruit, which are characteristics of the aperitif. Next, the young pineau is aged in either Limousin or Troncais oak, according to the style required, for a minimum of three years. Some pineau is aged for as long as ten years before bottling.

Pineau des Charentes is available in both white and red styles, and is marketed by about 600 producers, most of whom only operate on a small scale. Among the best-known names are Jules Robin and Château de Beaulon.

Christian Thomas in the Château de Beaulon distillery

CHATEAU
DE BEAULON

The Noble Aperitif

The Château de Beaulon was originally constructed in 1480, in the tiny village of Saint Dizant du Gua but it was not until 1712 that it was first used for growing vines by Louis-Amable de Bigot. Today, it is owned by Christian Thomas, who is regarded as one of the finest producers of Pineau des Charentes.

This outstanding example of pineau uses noble Bordeaux-grape varieties. Semillon and Sauvignon Blanc go into the making of its Pineau Blanc (white), and Cabernet Sauvignon, Cabernet Franc, and Merlot for its Pineau Rouge (red). Both styles are marketed at five and ten years of age. The cognac used is always distilled from the grapes picked in the château's own vineyards.

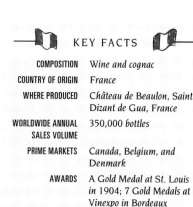

KEY FACTS

COMPOSITION	Wine and cognac
COUNTRY OF ORIGIN	France
WHERE PRODUCED	Château de Beaulon, Saint Dizant de Gua, France
WORLDWIDE ANNUAL SALES VOLUME	350,000 bottles
PRIME MARKETS	Canada, Belgium, and Denmark
AWARDS	A Gold Medal at St. Louis in 1904; 7 Gold Medals at Vinexpo in Bordeaux between 1980 and 1995
VISITORS	Visitors are welcome. Please telephone (33) 546499613

TO SERVE

The *five-year-old Château de Beaulon Pineau Blanc* has a light-golden color with an aromatic bouquet. It is very fruity, with a sweet finish.

The *five-year-old Château de Beaulon Pineau Rouge* has a soft-red color with a fruity bouquet. It is very round and soft on the palate, and has a complex, sweet aftertaste, on which fine cognac can be distinguished.

The *ten-year-old Château de Beaulon Vieille Réserve Or* has an intense-gold color, with fine cognac and vanilla evident on the nose. It is elegant on the palate, with citrus-style flavors followed by a lingering, sweet finish.

The *ten-year-old Château de Beaulon Vieille Réserve Ruby* has a mahogany color with a nose that contains hints of flowers and plums. It is very complex on the palate, and has a fairly rich, long finish.

All Pineau des Charentes should be served as follows:

☆ Chilled, not iced, in a tulip-shaped glass

For the Pineau Blanc Vieille Reserve Or, only white grapes – 80 percent Semillon and 20 percent Sauvignon Blanc – are used. The Pineau Rouge Vieille Reserve Ruby is a blend of Cabernet Franc (85 percent) and Merlot (15 percent). The white style is vinified in the usual pineau way, but is then aged for a minimum of ten years in specially selected, large-grained, Limousin-oak barrels. The red style is left in contact with the skins long enough to allow a full color and flavor to develop, and is also aged for ten years. During this time, its original purple color turns into a mahogany hue. After aging, the wine is blended, filtered, and bottled.

Château de Beaulon

164

PORT

The Portuguese-British Classic

The success of port as an international wine owes a great deal to the turbulent political situation that existed in seventeenth-century Europe. Although the title of "oldest port house" may belong to the Dutch-owned company of Kopke, which was founded in 1638, since then, the majority of houses have been either British or Portuguese. The oldest of the British-owned port houses, Warre, was founded in 1670, an important date for comprehending why the British became so active as port shippers: in the late 1660s, the French minister, Colbert, suddenly announced high taxes on the wines of Bordeaux, an act that resulted in a boycott of all Bordeaux wines. The Portuguese were quick to exploit the situation through the Methuen Treaty, which permitted favorable tax rates for the British, and for wines shipped to the British Isles from the Douro Valley.

Sandeman's Quinta do Vau in Douro

THE PORT WINE REGION

The port wine region is situated in northern Portugal in the valley of the river Douro. The vineyards begin about 50 miles east and inland of the city of Oporto – from which, according to tradition, the name "port" comes – and stretch along the river as far as the Spanish border. The wine is made upstream in the vineyards of *quintas*, or farms, in the middle and upper Douro, and then taken down to Oporto, where it is aged before being bottled and shipped. Almost all the port houses are not actually in Oporto itself, but on the opposite bank of the Douro estuary.

The evolution of red port, from ruby to tawny styles

For about three centuries, it was common practice for the wine to be left upstream until the spring after the vintage, when it was taken downstream in pipes on boats called *barcos rabelos*. (A *pipe* is an oak barrel with a capacity of around 114 to 121 gallons, which was originally made out of wood from a local tree known as the *pipas*.) In recent times, the tradition of transporting the wine down the Douro by boat has been replaced by road tankers that carry the wine in bulk to the port lodges on the estuary, where it is immediately put into pipes for aging and blending.

PORT AS AN APERITIF

For many consumers, port is the finest fortified wine of all, with its great concentration of flavor and superb structure. However, only white and tawny styles are really suitable as aperitifs.

Port has traditionally been a fortified wine made from red grapes, so when Stanley and Dick Yeatman of Taylor's, generally regarded as the Rolls Royce of port houses, made the first white port in 1935 and called it "Chip Dry," it came as something of a surprise to many of their competitors. But these days, any of the leading port houses are likely to offer a well-chilled glass of white port in warm weather.

PRODUCTION

Port is made from wine from a number of different grape varieties grown in the Douro Valley, and is fortified with neutral alcohol before being aged in oak pipes in large, above-ground, stone-built cellars called "lodges." Most white port is sold when two to three years of age, while good tawnies can vary from five years to Taylor's remarkable, 40-year-old example. Some cheaper tawnies are produced by blending pale, less-developed reds with white wines, but all the better tawnies are matured in the traditional manner, by taking selected red ports and leaving them in oak pipes until their color fades to tawny.

Sandeman and Taylor's both market attractive white ports that are quite widely available. Traditionally, all ports were aged in oak pipes, but recently, some white ports have been stored either in large, oak vats, or in giant, stainless-steel vats. The use of stainless steel, in particular, has helped to produce a new generation of white ports that are much fresher and livelier in character than those of 20 years ago.

TO SERVE PORT

Both tawny and white ports should always be served chilled, or at least cellar-cool. White port blends well with most long mixers. Younger tawnies, under 10 years, can be delicious with ice. Neither of these styles requires decanting, and both are ready to drink when purchased.

Oak casks in the Sandeman aging lodges

TAYLOR'S
Chip Dry
PORT
FINEST EXTRA DRY WHITE

Estd. 1692

Product of Portugal - Bottled by
TAYLOR, FLADGATE & YEATMAN VINHOS S.A. - OPORTO
Established 1692

SANDEMAN PORT

Old Cauliflower Ears

In 1790, George Sandeman left Perth in Scotland for the City of London, and began trading in port from a somewhat disreputable establishment called Tom's Coffee House. He is reputed to have been the first person to ship a vintage port in 1791, and a few years later, he extended his activities to shipping sherry. He was known as "Old Cauliflower Ears" because of his eccentric appearance and protruding ears.

Sandeman is best known for its popular blended ports, and two of these, Sandeman White Port and Sandeman Imperial Tawny, are ideal as aperitifs. Sandeman White Port is produced from white grapes, using the latest in modern wine-making techniques. The juice is fermented in temperature-controlled, stainless-steel vats to

 KEY FACTS

COMPOSITION	Wine from the delimited vineyards of the Douro Valley, and neutral grape alcohol
COUNTRY OF ORIGIN	Portugal
WHERE PRODUCED	Douro Valley, Portugal
PRIME MARKETS	France, Belgium, USA, UK, and Japan
VISITORS	Sandeman has an excellent visitor center alongside its head office on the quayside in Vila Nova de Gaia. It also has a visitor facility upstream in the Douro Valley. Contact João on: (351-2) 3706816

retain the fresh, fruity flavors, and the wine is then fortified to 20 percent alcohol by volume (abv).

Sandeman Imperial Tawny is a superior, well-aged tawny produced from Touriga Nacional, Touriga Francesca, Tinta Roriz, Tinta Barocca, and Tinta Cão grapes, which are grown either in Sandeman's own vineyards, or on the farms of growers who have supplied the company for generations.

TO SERVE

Sandeman White Port *has a pale-straw color, with a fresh, vinous bouquet. It gives a crisp, lively tang on the palate, and has a refreshing aftertaste.*
It should be served as follows:

☆ *Well chilled, on its own*

☆ *On ice*

☆ *On ice, with tonic and a slice of lemon*

☆ *On ice, with white lemonade*

Sandeman Imperial Tawny *has a rich, tawny color, with a mature, vinous bouquet. It lingers on the palate, and has delicious, tropical-fruit flavors.*
It is best served as follows:

☆ *On its own*

☆ *On its own, well chilled*

TAYLOR'S PORT

The Family-Owned House

This great port house, widely known as Taylor's, is officially registered as Taylor, Fladgate & Yeatman, a name it acquired as a partnership in 1844. It was originally founded by Job Bearsley in 1692, and the first Taylor joined in 1816, but no-one of that name survived to the end of the nineteenth century. The company is now jointly owned by Alistair Robertson, Huyshe Bower, and Bruce Guimarens. Its outstanding personality was Frank "Smiler" Yeatman, who was a partner for 53 years (1897–1950), and who personally took charge of 50 different harvests. Taylor's is still a family-owned house, and is proud of its independence.

Few port lovers would dispute that the range of four tawnies produced by Taylor's is unique. Taylor's 10-, 20-, 30-, and 40-year-old tawnies are blended wines, and the figures given represent their average ages, or the amount of time the wines have spent in oak pipes since the grapes

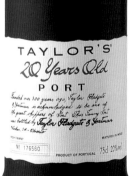

 KEY FACTS

COMPOSITION	Wine and neutral grape brandy
COUNTRY OF ORIGIN	Portugal
WHERE PRODUCED	Douro Valley, Portugal
PRIME MARKETS	UK, USA, France
AWARDS	Numerous, but unspecified
VISITORS	Visitors are welcome at Rua do Choupeza 250, Vila Nova de Gaia, Portugal. Telephone: (351-2) 3919999

were originally pressed. The labels state the age of each tawny and the actual year of bottling, and all the wines are ready for immediate consumption. Tawny ports, unlike vintage ports, do not improve in the bottle.

TO SERVE

Taylor's "Chip Dry" has a light-gold color with a fresh, vinous bouquet. It is quite tangy on the palate, with a lingering finish that is slightly sweet. It is best served as follows:

☆ On ice, in a tumbler

☆ Tall, with tonic, soda water, or lemonade

Taylor's 10-Year-Old Tawny is one of the deepest-colored tawnies, and has a mature, vinous aroma. It is surprisingly youthful on the palate, with a rich, mellow, raisiny aftertaste.

Taylor's 20-Year-Old Tawny has a more traditional tawny color, a fine and elegant bouquet, and a delicious balance of fruit and acidity, followed by a long, nutty, almost honeyed aftertaste. Both are best served as follows:

☆ Slightly chilled, in a small port glass

☆ On ice (in warm weather)

☆ At room temperature (in cool weather)

Taylor's 30-Year-Old Tawny is at an age where there can be some variations in color, but it often has a lighter, tawny-orange color. It is a truly fine, extremely well-balanced wine, with an elegant aroma and a complex aftertaste. Taylor's 30-Year-Old should be served as follows:

☆ At room temperature only, in a port glass

The only "digital" technology employed at vintage time at Taylor's are the pickers' fingers and treaders' toes, as the company still insists that the original, traditional way of making port is

Grapes ready for pressing

the best. In all its literature, the house asserts that "no machines can yet match the sensitivity of the human hand, eye, or foot." It supports this statement by hand-picking its grapes and treading them in stone *lagares* (granite tanks). At the appropriate moment, when the fermentation process has converted approximately half the natural sugar into alcohol, a neutral grape brandy is added to fortify the port to around 20 percent abv (alcohol by volume). This immediately stops the fermentation, and retains much of the original sweetness from the ripe grapes.

All fine tawnies start life as ruby ports – that is, as bright red, young fortified wines that are placed in oak pipes to mature. During the aging process, their color is gradually absorbed by the oak, and becomes tawny. Very few houses can market such old tawnies as Taylor's, because it is necessary to possess extensive stocks of old wines for blending and for replenishing.

White port is ideal chilled

SHERRY

The Frontier's Finest Wine

Sherry is a dry, white wine made from the Palomino-grape variety and fortified with neutral-grape brandy. Both the wine and the brandy must come from the officially demarcated Jerez region, whose vineyards were among the earliest to be cultivated in western Europe. The wine is usually sweetened by adding a sticky, dark-brown wine called PX, the abbreviated name of the Pedro Ximenez grape variety. Occasionally, a sweet moscatel-grape variety is used.

Production is centered on the town of Jerez de la Frontera, which lies just south of Seville, and from which the English name

Sherry vineyards

"sherry" is derived. The region has one of the warmest vineyard climates in Europe, which led some of the local producers to adopt night-time harvesting as early as 1875. Nowadays, night-time harvesting is practiced in many vineyards in the New-World countries, as crushing the grapes when their juice is at its coolest has proven to give superior results.

The Palomino variety gives its best results in Jerez, where it supplies 90 percent of the grapes, and also produces many fine wines, with a sprinkling of truly great ones. Pedro Ximenez is much more widely planted in other regions of southern Spain, where it is used mainly to make an inexpensive, dry white wine, while in the Jerez region its function is purely as a sweetening and coloring agent. The third variety, moscatel, is only grown on a small scale in Jerez, and acts as a sweetener. It is a synonym for Muscat d'Alexandria, a variety popular for fortified wines in Australia, South Africa, Greece, France, and other parts of Spain.

PRODUCTION

Much of the mystique of sherry production can be traced to the long, tall, cathedral-like cellars called *bodegas* that were first designed some centuries ago to keep the wine cool while it is aged in butts. It is within these *bodegas* that *flor* occurs, completely spontaneously, on the

Palomino fino grapes

surface of most of the young wines, about two months after the pressing. Within a month, it develops into a slightly off-white film, about a tenth of an inch in depth. *Flor* feeds upon the remaining grape sugars, glycerine, and volatile acids, and encourages the growth of esthers and aldehydes. In effect, it makes a sherry drier, giving it that unique, slightly yeasty taste, that when combined with the characteristics of the *Albariza* soil, provides it with its distinctive flavor. Its conduct intrigued bacteriologist Alexander Fleming, who, while carrying out his research on penicillin in the 1920s, visited the *bodegas* of Pedro Domecq in order to observe the behavior of *flor*. *Flor* seems to flourish in the sea air, since it grows more profusely in the *bodegas* of the coastal towns of Puerto de

Tio Pepe's Bodega Las Copas

Santa Maria and Sanlucar than in Jerez de la Frontera. The sherries on which *flor* settles substantially will develop into finos or manzanillas, the naturally drier styles. The others will turn into the rarely seen but delicious *palo cortado*, or the full-bodied *oloroso*. Unprotected by *flor*, these sherries undergo oxidation before turning a darker color. They also develop a higher alcohol level.

Both the aging and blending of sherries is done using the solera system. Long rows of sherry butts are stacked four levels high. Wine for bottling is always taken from the butts at ground level, then replaced by sherry from the row above, then replenished with sherry from the third row, and the third row with wine from the top level, which is finally restocked with new sherry.

THE DIFFERENT SHERRY STYLES

FINO

Fino is considered by many as *the* classic sherry style, and should always be drunk well chilled. In the Jerez region, the entire local sherry consumption consists almost exclusively of *fino* or *manzanilla*. *Fino* is normally a light-straw color, and is the most elegant and delicate of sherry styles, with a fresh bouquet and dry palate. In southern Spain, it is a regular accompaniment to both tapas and shellfish. Elsewhere, it is usually served as an aperitif, especially with nuts and olives. Many sherry houses regard their principal *fino* as their

Grapes in the lagar ready for vinification

flagship. Gonzalez Byass Tio Pepe, Pedro Domecq La Ina, and Garvey San Patricio are leading examples of *finos* that have become brands in their own right.

MANZANILLA

Manzanilla is a *fino* that has been produced in the sub-region of Sanlucar de Barrameda. Its salty tang is said to be due to the proximity of the *bodegas* to the Atlantic. Manzanilla is more restricted in volume, and is less-well known to the layman, and subsequently its labels are less familiar than those of the leading *finos*. Hidalgo la Gitana, Delgado Zuleta La Goya, La Guita, Williams & Humbert, Allegria, and Barbadillo are all successful.

OLOROSO

Oloroso is Spanish for "fragrant." As a young wine, an *oloroso* soon develops a darker color than a *fino*, due to the non-existence of *flor* on its surface and the subsequent oxidation. It is a naturally dry style, and is often blended with Pedro Ximenez to make medium-dry to sweet sherries. An *oloroso* is considerably fuller than a *fino*, and generally has more body than an *amontillado*. This firmer structure means that often an *oloroso* will last longer in the bottle than other styles. As sherry expert Julian Jeffs noted, Manuel Gonzalez Gordon of Gonzalez Byass acutely assessed three styles in a nutshell by comparing *"fino* to an almond, *amontillado* to a hazelnut, and *oloroso* to a walnut." Gonzalez Byass Matusalem Muy Viejo, which means "very old Methusaleh," from the oldest man in the Bible, is a very old, long-aged, sweetened *oloroso* that is widely regarded as the finest example of that particular style. It is fairly expensive, but memorable. Emilio Lustau Almacenista Dry Oloroso and Emilio Lustau Rich Old Oloroso are also remarkable.

AMONTILLADO

The term *amontillado* first appeared in the second half of the eighteenth century. The reason seems to be the *amontillado* style's similarity in character to the wines of Montilla, though some doubt arises, as the latter are not fortified. There is some dispute concerning the use of the word. Sherry afficionados claim that an *amontillado* is a *fino* that has been aged in wood for at least eight years. However, there are many brands of *amontillado* that are aged in wood for less than four years. The traditional style should have a deep, golden color, a nutty bouquet, and a full, dry, mature taste. It will also cost about twice as much as a commercial blend. Nowadays, commercial brands produce economically priced, relatively young *amontillados*, which have been sweetened at least to medium to suit the popular palate. Among the more popular *amontillado* sherries are Emilio Lustau Fine Dry Amontillado, Gonzalez Byass La Concha, Croft Particular Pale Amontillado, Don Ramos, and Harvey's Club.

PALO CORTADO

Palo cortado is one of the most confusing styles to describe as, unfortunately, the Jerez region is not united in its definition. Some say that it is an *oloroso*, which resembles a *fino* in character; others say that it is an *oloroso* in the style of an *amontillado*. Some sherry houses actually sell *palo cortado* when it is only a few years old, while many experts maintain that it takes many years to develop. *Palo cortado* is the one style that develops neither as a *flor*-covered *fino* nor a clear-surfaced *oloroso*. Occasionally, it attracts a little *flor*, but it is usually darker than *finos* and *olorosos*, has a full bouquet, and a crisp finish. Gonzalez Byass and Emilio Lustau produce distinguished *palo cortado* sherries.

A venenciador serves sherry the traditional way

CREAM SHERRIES

Cream sherries have been blended, and range in color from pale- to rich-cream or nut-brown in color. When visiting the Harvey's *bodega* in the late 1980s, it was quite surprising to learn that, contrary to what I had read, Harvey's Bristol Cream, the world's No. 1 sherry, "is a blend of *finos* and *olorosos*, without the addition of any Pedro Ximenez." Yet, in the late nineteenth century, when an aristocratic French lady, a customer of Harvey's, first identified one of their sherries as a "Bristol Cream," she was told it was a straight *oloroso*!

DARK SHERRIES

There are also nut-brown and dark-brown sherries, whose color comes from adding *Vino de Color*, a sticky, natural syrup. This is made by taking unfermented grape juice and concentrating it over a slow fire in a copper cauldron.

CROFT
PALE CREAM SHERRY

The Innovators

The House of Croft was founded in Oporto in 1676, when it was known as Phayre and Bradley. It did not become involved in the sherry market until 1970, when it opened superb new *bodegas* on the outskirts of Jerez de la Frontera. Croft astonished the existing houses by introducing the first-ever, pale-cream sherry. Some of the more-traditional sherry producers were critical of this new style, which they rather harshly judged as not a real sherry. They were also censorious of the bottle shape, which didn't conform to local custom. In subsequent years, sales of many of the long-established sherry houses have declined steadily, while Croft has captured a huge market.

 KEY FACTS

COMPOSITION	*Wine, possibly mistelle, and Brandy de Jerez*
COUNTRY OF ORIGIN	*Spain*
WHERE PRODUCED	*Rancho Croft, Jerez de la Frontera, Spain*
PRIME MARKETS	*UK, Republic of Ireland, Spain*
AWARDS	*Gold medals at the Spanish Wine Olympics, 1976 and The International Wine and Spirit Competition, London 1990*
VISITORS	*Visits by private invitation only*

Croft is still somewhat secretive about its product. Possibly, in making its Original style, Croft uses some moscatel wine, the third approved grape variety in the official Jerez region, adding a *mistelle* from the same grape variety. Like all sherries, Croft Pale Cream is fortified using the same neutral, local brandy. The blending and aging take from four to five years.

Croft also produces a pale, medium-dry, amontillado sherry called Particular. It is lighter and drier in taste than Croft Original Pale Cream. However, Croft's finest sherry is produced in small quantities: Croft Limited Edition, which is only sold in half bottles, is a very old, pale-cream sherry that has a golden hue and a distinctive palate. The average age of the wines in its blend is 12 years.

Vineyard with bodega in the background

TO SERVE

Croft has a very pale straw color, an attractive fresh nose, a sweet palate, a very smooth finish, and a refreshing aftertaste.
All Croft styles should be served as follows:

☆ Well chilled

☆ With ice

☆ With ice, and tonic

DOMECQ LA INA

The Irish-Basque Connection

On reflection, it is not so surprising that the celebrated sherry house of Pedro Domecq was in fact founded by an Irish horse dealer called Paddy Murphy in 1730 – both Andalusia and Ireland have been famed for horse breeding for centuries, and in the 1700s, trade flourished between the two. It was another couple of generations before Pedro Domecq, a French citizen of Basque heritage, inherited a share of the business, and changed the trading name accordingly. His successors established the La Ina solera in 1922.

The name "*La Ina,*" according to the late José Ignacio Domecq, derived from the Moorish battle cry "*Aina,*" and referred to a favorite place of his for hare coursing, where he used to enjoy a chilled glass of his finest *fino* sherry before the chase.

 KEY FACTS

COMPOSITION	Flor, dry white wine from 100 percent Palomino grapes, and purified grape-alcohol from the official Brandy de Jerez denomination
COUNTRY OF ORIGIN	Spain
WHERE PRODUCED	Jerez de la Frontera, Spain
PRIME MARKETS	Spain, UK, Netherlands
AWARDS	Royal warrant of Her Majesty Queen Elizabeth II of England
VISITORS	Visitor center in Jerez. Telephone: (34-56) 151500

The grapes are picked by hand in September, and after pressing, the juice is stored in vats, where it is allowed to ferment until all the grape sugar has been converted into alcohol – which may be any time between the following January and March. The wine is then filtered to ensure clarity, and fortified with neutral-grape alcohol before being transferred to oak butts in the Domecq *bodegas*. By July, *flor* has begun to develop on the surface of the sherry, and after a year, it is transferred to a solera, where it is aged and blended before being bottled for marketing. Domecq La Ina is the second best-selling *fino* in worldwide terms.

TO SERVE

La Ina is a pale-straw color, with a fresh bouquet and a slightly yeasty aroma. It is crisp and delicious on the palate, with a pleasing tang and a fine, long finish.
Domecq La Ina should be served as follows:

☆ *Well chilled, in a half-filled copita, on its own, or with tapas*

Palomino grapes

GONZALEZ BYASS
TIO PEPE

Uncle's Favorite Drink

Tio Pepe – which means "Uncle Joe" – owes its origins to the gratitude of a fatherless boy, whose health was so poor that he was not expected to survive into adulthood. The boy, Manuel Gonzalez Angel, lived in Seville with his widowed mother, and seven brothers and sisters, but was cared for by his uncle Joe, who traded in *manzanilla* wines in the port of Sanlucar. Against the odds, Manuel's health improved, and when he became an adult, he settled in Jerez, and began exporting all styles of sherry. Tio Pepe was a frequent visitor to Manuel's cellars, and he singled out one particular butt of *fino* as his personal favorite. As Manuel was only too delighted to ensure that his uncle's favorite

 KEY FACTS

COMPOSITION	Palomino grapes and neutral-grape brandy
COUNTRY OF ORIGIN	Spain
WHERE PRODUCED	Gonzalez Byass, Jerez de la Frontera, Spain
WORLDWIDE ANNUAL SALES VOLUME	Nine million bottles
PRIME MARKETS	Spain, UK, USA
AWARDS	In 1862, Queen Isabel of Spain ordered that Tio Pepe be served every day at the Spanish court.
VISITORS	Tours at 10:00 a.m., 11:00 a.m., and midday everyday. Contact Consuelo Garcia Tuuio. Telephone: (34-56) 340000

sherry was always available to him, he had "Tio Pepe" stenciled on the butt.

News spread of this elegant *fino*. Soon, there were two butts of Tio Pepe, and so the tradition grew. Today, Uncle Joe's love for his nephew is immortalized through this top-selling, world-renowned sherry.

Tio Pepe, the world's favorite *fino* sherry, is a classic aperitif made from 100 percent pal-omino grapes from the official Jerez region, fortified to 15.5 percent abv (alcohol by volume) by adding grape brandy. It is made by the solera system, and aged for an average of seven years.

TO SERVE

Tio Pepe has a deep-straw color with a pungent, slightly yeasty bouquet. It is full, beautifully balanced, and almost nutty-tasting, with a crisp, dry finish. Tio Pepe should be served as follows:

☆ Well chilled, preferably in a copita — the classic, tulip-shaped aperitif glass

Manuel Gonzalez Angel

HARVEY'S
BRISTOL CREAM

The Cream of Bristol Milk

T he port of Bristol, in the southwest of England, became important to the wine-shipping trade when it was used as an alternative route for wines from Spain and Portugal that could avoid the English Channel at a time of persistent hostilities between the English and the French. Consequently, sherry became extremely popular, and one particularly sweet style developed, called "Bristol Milk." This was a generic term to denote that the sherry had been shipped through Bristol by a merchant with cellars there. One day, during the 1880s, an aristocratic French lady customer of John Harvey & Sons attended a tasting in their Denmark Street premises, near Bristol harbor. She was

 KEY FACTS

COMPOSITION	*Wine and young grape brandy*
COUNTRY OF ORIGIN	*Spain*
WHERE PRODUCED	*Jerez de la Frontera, Spain*
WORLDWIDE ANNUAL SALES VOLUME	*Approximately 10 million bottles*
PRIME MARKETS	UK, USA
AWARDS	A Gold Medal in the International Wine & Spirit Competition, London 1995
VISITORS	*Visitors are welcome at Harvey's quaint wine museum at 12 Denmark Street, Bristol, England.* Telephone: (44-117) 9275000

offered various cask samples of Bristol Milk before enquiring about another barrel of a richer, more full-bodied sherry. She was so impressed on trying it that she is reputed to have remarked, "If that was the milk, then this must be the cream!" And so Harvey's Bristol Cream was born, as John Harvey seized on her statement and registered it as a unique trademark, which no other producer is allowed to use. From that chance beginning, Harvey's Bristol Cream has grown into the top-selling sherry brand of

TO SERVE

Harvey's *Bristol Cream* has a deep-amber color, and a rich, pungent bouquet. It is full and sweet on the palate, and leaves a ripe, raisiny aftertaste.
Harvey's *Bristol Cream* should be served as follows:

☆ Chilled, on its own, in a sherry copita glass

☆ On ice, in a tumbler

This last method of serving is quite revolutionary to the sherry world, and has been especially promoted by Harvey's.

all. In the mid-1990s, Harvey's surprised both consumers and the wine trade by repackaging the Bristol Cream – which had previously been sold in brown bottles – in a blue-glass bottle, reviving the old tradition from the eighteenth century, when a Bristol merchant had exclusive rights to import Saxon smalt for glassmaking. This smalt contained cobalt, which provided a unique color when combined with English lead glass that came to

be known as Bristol Blue.

Harvey's Bristol Cream is made by first pressing Palomino and Pedro Ximenez grapes, and then fortifying the wine with young Brandy de Jerez. It is then aged and blended in a solera. Harvey's system of maturing the Pedro Ximenez wine in a solera is unique in the Jerez region, as most other houses simply make it in vats.

SANDEMAN SHERRY

A 200-Year-Old Business

George Sandeman

S hortly after the founder of the house, George Sandeman, began trading in port wine in 1790, the growing interest in sherry came to his attention, so he traveled to Jerez de la Frontera to make shipping arrangements. The development of his business coincided with the ascendancy of Napoleon, when many countries who were hostile to French imperialism began shipping sherry and port for two reasons: the unavailability of French wine, and a strong reluctance to trade with the French.

 KEY FACTS

COMPOSITION	Flor, white wine, and neutral-grape alcohol from the official Jerez region
COUNTRY OF ORIGIN	Spain
WHERE PRODUCED	Jerez de la Frontera, Spain
PRIME MARKETS	Germany, The Netherlands, Belgium, USA, and Japan
AWARDS	The royal warrant to Her Majesty Queen Elizabeth II of England
VISITORS	Sandeman has a popular visitor center at Jerez de la Frontera. Contact Ms. Pilar Muñoz; Telephone: (34-56) 303534

Sandeman Don Fino is made from 100 percent palomino grapes, and fortified with neutral-grape brandy.

The exact winemaking technique for Sandeman Soleo is believed to involve palomino and moscatel grapes.

Sandeman Character is a medium-dry amontillado.

Sandeman Armada Cream is a blend of *olorosos* and PX wine.

TO SERVE

Sandeman Don Fino *is a classic fino with the color of straw, a fine, yeasty nose, and a crisp, elegant finish.*

Sandeman Character *is a rich, amber-colored, medium-dry amontillado, and is extremely smooth and easy on the palate.*

Sandeman Soléo *is a recent introduction to the range, and is described as "Very Special Dry." It is an interesting attempt to market sherry in a clear, white-glass bottle so that its pale-golden color is visible.*

Sandeman Armada Cream *is a traditional cream sherry that is particularly popular in colder climates, where the sweeter styles of many drinks are in demand.*

All Sandeman sherries – with the exception of the darkest and oldest special blends – can be served as follows:

The traditional way:
☆ *Chilled*

The modernist way:
☆ *On ice (this works well with cream sherries)*

The revolutionary way:
☆ *With ice, and tonic (mainly for* finos*)*
☆ *With ice, and lemonade (mainly for* finos*)*

VALDESPINO
INOCENTE

Aged in a Monastery

The 500-year-old house of Valdespino markets the highly rated "Inocente Fino," which they describe as "the only single-vineyard sherry." It is aged uniquely by using 10 scales in its solera, rather than the usual four.

Apart from the 10-scale solera system, Valdespino Inocente is made like any other *fino*, that is, by making a dry white wine from 100 percent palomino grapes, and then fortifying it with Jerez brandy. It attracts *flor* during its aging, which usually takes place over a period of five years.

 KEY FACTS

COMPOSITION	*Wine and young-grape brandy*
COUNTRY OF ORIGIN	*Spain*
WHERE PRODUCED	*Jerez de la Frontera, Spain*
WORLDWIDE ANNUAL SALES VOLUME	*Valdespino's total sales are 400,000 bottles per annum. Valdespino Inocente represents a small fraction of that*
PRIME MARKETS	*UK, USA, The Netherlands*
AWARDS	*Gold Medals in Madrid 1877, Dublin 1892, and Amsterdam 1895*

WILLIAMS & HUMBERT
DRY SACK SHERRY

A Family Partnership

I n 1876, two brothers-in-law, Alexander Williams and Arthur Humbert, formed a partnership, and began trading under their joint names as sherry producers and shippers. Alexander Williams already had some experience of sherry production, so he operated from Jerez de la Frontera, while Arthur Humbert ran their London office. In 1906, Carl Williams, a second-generation partner, launched a new brand of sherry called "Dry Sack," literally packaging it in a hessian-covered bottle. The word "sack," as used in wine terms, actually has no connection with any bottle style, but comes from a drink that was at that time called "Sherris Sack," a full-bodied and very sweet wine. Also, "Sack" was widely used in Spanish territory for export wines such as Malaga Sack and Canary Sack. Nearly a

KEY FACTS

COMPOSITION	*Wine and a neutral Brandy de Jerez*
COUNTRY OF ORIGIN	*Spain*
WHERE PRODUCED	*Jerez de la Frontera, Spain*
WORLDWIDE ANNUAL SALES VOLUME	*Williams & Humbert produce over 12 million bottles of sherry; exact figures for Dry Sack are unavailable*
PRIME MARKETS	*The Netherlands, UK, and Germany*
VISITORS	*Visitors are welcome. Telephone: (34-56) 346539*

century later, Williams & Humbert have taken another innovative step by making their Dry Sack a medium-dry. Currently, Williams & Humbert is part of the Spanish-Dutch company, Luis Páez S.A.

Dry Sack is a blend of amontillado and oloroso sherries with a Pedro Ximenez wine. The latter is quite unusual, in that Pedro Ximenez grapes are pressed to make a single-varietal fortified wine, which is then blended with the first two styles. Dry Sack is fortified to 20.5 percent abv (alcohol by volume), but this varies depending on its destination in the international markets. Dry Sack spends an average of eight years aging in its solera, which contains traces of wines that date back to the last century.

TO SERVE

Dry Sack has a bright-amber hue, and a delicate, fragrant bouquet. It has a slightly raisiny taste, and is very smooth on the palate, with a medium-dry finish.

Williams & Humbert produce three other sherries of note: Pando, a crisp, dry fino; Dos Cortados, which is a palo cortado with a deep, oak-like taste; and A Winter's Tale, which is practically a dessert wine.

Dry Sack and similar sherries should be served as follows:

☆ Well chilled

☆ On ice

Dry Sack is best served in either traditional Spanish copitas or in tulip-shaped wine glasses.

INDEX

PICTURE CREDITS

Abbreviations: pp = pages; b = bottom; l = left; r = right; t = top.

Allied Domecq: pp180, 181. Aperol: pp7, 58. Archive Photos France: 18. Barbero:p45.
Berger:p62r. Blandy's:p22. Campari:pp27, 28, 35, 37t, 38, 42, 43t, 47t, 67, 68, 69, 70, 71l.
Castillo de Lira: p158. Chateau de Beaulon: p162, 164. Cinzano: pp74, 75r, 78, 79.
CIVDN: pp25, 137l. Cocchi: p81. Croft: p179l. Distilleries et Domaines de Provence:
p161. e.t. Archive: pp6, 13, 29. Florio: pp24, 147, 150. Garden/Wildlife Matters: p94.
Gonzalez Byass: pp20, 174b, 183. Harry's Bar: p49. Harvey's: p185.Heaven Hill Company:
p86r. Janet Price: p157. The Madeira Wine Institute: pp138, 141. Marie Brizard: p32.
Martini: pp11, 14, 15, 16, 36, 37t, 40, 41, 96t, 98, 99. Noilly Prat: pp17, 101. Pellegrino:
p152. Perez Barquero: pp33, 153, 154, 156. Pernod-Ricard: 9, 54, 65, 118, 127. Picon:
pp39, 111. Pimm's: p73. Port Wine Institute: pp23b, 173t. Portuguese Tourist Office:
p160. Punt e Mes: p115. Riccadonna: pp119, 121. Routin: p73. St Raphael: pp19, 125.
Sandeman: pp21, 37b, 43b, 165, 166, 167l, 169t, 173, 174t, 175, 186t, 177. SIVIR: pp133,
136, 137r. Sopexa: p26. Spanish Tourist Office: p144. Taylor's: p172b. Trevor Wood: p46r.
Warninks: 128, 129. Williams and Humbert: p189.